MARK ROLLINS
and the
Puppeteer

ISBN: 0-9825898-0-8
ISBN-13: 9780982589809
Library of Congress Control Number: 2009910033

Visit markrollinsadventures.com.
Cover Design by Tom Trebing.

Also by M. Thomas (Tom) Collins

Mark Rollins and the Rainmaker
Mark Rollins' New Career & the Women's Health Club
Marion Collins Remembers Old Sayings and Lessons for Life

MARK ROLLINS and the Puppeteer

Tom Collins

The Puppeteer is a story of murder in the law firm. While this mystery is a work of fiction, the destructive issues of embezzlement and eat-what-you-kill compensation plans, all too prevalent in law firms, are the real stuff. I trust that the result is both entertaining and educational, especially for those in the legal community.

In preparing to write this Mark Rollins adventure, I made four new friends—Rick, Janelle, Angela, and Blake, the team at Uselton Arms gun store and shooting range in Franklin, Tennessee. Their gun knowledge and skills helped me tell a better story. Thank you, guys. I also owe a special thanks to my mentor, Al Thomason, whose attention to detail as a volunteer editor made the story more readable. As usual, my loving wife's input and especially her help with character names always makes for a more honest story. ⟿

"About Me"

My name is Mark Rollins. I am a senior citizen. My driver's license lists my height as 5'9", my eyes as blue, and my hair as brown. However, the brown is now largely gray, and I gave up the comb-over for a military-style buzz cut. I have the body type of a defensive linebacker, and I work out regularly in an effort to stay younger than my years. Except when necessity dictates otherwise, I wear my trademark personal uniform—khaki trousers, black cotton polo, and Cole Haan driving shoes. I drink martinis, straight up with an olive, and prefer Skyy or Belvedere vodka. I am a cancer survivor and living proof of the adage "what doesn't kill me makes me stronger." I am also in the fortunate position of having access to powerful people in high places and of being rather wealthy. In fact, money just keeps rolling in. What I don't spend or invest in pet projects, I just turn over to the professional wealth management team at Goldman Sachs where it becomes little more than numbers on a computer screen.

As for how I got to where I am, the money originated from the business side of my life. After starting my career as a CPA, I invested in the birth of the computer industry with several companies that went public and built my initial high net worth. Then in 1986, I started a high-tech company, Themis Legal Software, to develop software specifically for law firms. Within twenty years, a third of all U.S. law firms were using Themis software, and I was considered an expert on the profitable operation of the modern law firm. I wrote articles, gave presentations, and hosted an award-winning blog read by most law firm managing partners. In 2007, I sold Themis to a large international corporation and retired—at least, I *intended* to retire. It didn't work out that way.

My access to powerful people and a penchant for adventure came from another side of my life. It began in the early 1990s when the U.S. government asked me to help fledgling technology enterprises in Eastern Europe. Our government had decided emerging technology in that part of the world was in our national interest. Unfortunately, governments outside the West feared technology in private hands, especially the Internet and its World Wide Web. The fortunes of start-up businesses were also at risk from criminal gangs that were infiltrating those emerging private enterprises. More than once, my wife, Sarah, and I became the targets of villainous people out to do us harm.

It took more than my know-how and the vision of those courageous Eastern European entrepreneurs to advance global technology in their part of the world. It also took my access to the forces of the U.S. government to crush those who would prevent or preempt its advance.

A word about Sarah... she has been described has a blue jean-wearing grandmother with a mean temper. She has a fondness for antique hand axes. You won't find her collection on display. But, she knows where each and every axe is hidden, and she can reach one in a flash. Sarah knows how to protect herself and, if a threat calls for it, she knows how to take the offense. Now days Sarah spends most of her time taking care of the Rollins family compound, helping with the grandchildren, or working in her gardens. But she didn't always. Sarah was a career marketing executive. She was the "big idea" person behind some of the most successful advertising campaigns in our country. Even today when she discovers a product or service that delivers on its intended purpose, a rarity, she can't help mentally designing a new campaign for it. Occasionally she will call the ad agency handling an account to offer them her ideas. There are very few agencies worth their salt that don't know who Sarah Rollins is. They know that when Sarah calls, they need to listen.

My retirement plans were derailed when, for reasons beyond explanation, I became the owner of the Women's Health Club located in the Brentwood suburb of Nashville, Tennessee. The WH Club, as most people call it, is an exclusive ladies-only facility for socially elite and wealthy women. It is a place where they can work hard to keep their seductive figures and hang on to a youthful appearance. The Club started simply as an exclusive fitness facility and expanded over time to include just about everything our rich female members wanted or needed. We have resident divorce lawyers, discreet private banking (including lockboxes), a platonic escort service, top hair and makeup artists, a nip and tuck department, wardrobe consultant, expert fitting and tailoring professionals, a shopping service, car service, tanning facility, and more. You name it—if our club members will pay for it, we add it to our menu of services and usually bill for those extras under the heading "Miscellaneous Expenses".

I have people who take care of the details of running the fitness club side of the business. My role has become that of a father figure to our ladies—the club members. When they are troubled or upset for any reason, including difficulties in their personal lives, they come to me. I make things right. I make their problems go away. It is strictly legal… or, I should say, I never *seriously* break the law.

CHAPTER 1

The Murder

My morning newspaper was already on the breakfast table thanks to our new live-in help, Dorin and his wife, Gabriela. They migrated here from Romania. Dorin is a graduate student at Vanderbilt and the couple needed a place to stay. My wife, Sarah, was ready to let someone else do the cooking, at least for a while, and I was happy to have someone else changing the light bulbs and doing the other "man around the house" duties required to keep the family compound in fine fettle.

Unfortunately, I could not enjoy Gabriela's wonderful breakfast. The front-page headline over the photograph of Harold T. Lansden, Esq. read "Belle Meade Attorney Murdered." Harold Lansden, H.T. to his friends, was the senior partner in the law firm of Lansden, Tillman and Hall. The Lansdens have been prominent in the Nashville

legal community for over 200 years. Their name carries
a lot of weight and there had been an expectation that
H.T. would not spend his life practicing law. He had his
sights set on the Governor's Mansion, but no one expected
that to satisfy his political ambitions. Harold was fond
of saying, "I'm the fourth generation of Lansdens in
Tennessee. Four is my lucky number. So far, we have had
three Presidents from Tennessee. That means there is an
opening for number four!"

H.T. wore his success well. He was just short of six
feet tall on a frame that could double as a men's store
mannequin. He passed up the usual dark blue suit and
French-cuffed shirts worn by cut-from-the-mold national
politicians. Instead, he usually wore perfectly tailored gray
suits. His custom-made shirts were obligatory white but
with straight collars and buttoned sleeves. It was the dress
uniform of a highly confident and successful individual
rather than that of a *wannabe*. It was a style deliberately
intended to put others at ease.

H.T.'s law office location was unique but appropriate
for 200 years of Nashville legal history. While most of
the larger local law firms had moved to the upper floors of
the city's skyscrapers, the offices of Lansden, Tillman and
Hall occupied one of the historic brownstone buildings
with an entrance on both Fourth Avenue and Nashville's
notorious Printers Alley.

The Alley is home to some of Nashville's more bawdy
nightlife. In its heyday, it was strictly the Men's Quarter
where the local police unofficially condoned illegal
gambling, liquor, and ladies of the night. Back then, the

ground floor of the building housing H.T.'s law firm was the Alley's most elegant saloon. The opulence wasn't limited to the saloon. An upscale bordello occupied the building's private upper floors attracting the state's and city's most powerful men among its customers, including the governor, the mayor, and the police chief. H.T.'s building, only blocks from the State Capitol of Tennessee and Nashville's courthouse, is also home to one of Nashville's famous ghosts, Rocky Johnson, who killed himself with a shot to the head when the saloon and whorehouse he managed was finally shut down in 1916. To this day, Rocky is said to torment building occupants by moving things around and making midnight appearances when young associates or paralegals work into the early morning hours to meet a pressure-filled deadline.

According to the story in *The Tennessean,* Harold T. Lansden was gunned down by an unknown assailant last night around ten o'clock when he left his office. As for a motive, the article suggested that his death was unintentional. Witnesses on the scene described the shooter as an extremely intoxicated male who had fired a weapon in celebratory fashion and accidentally ended the life of Tennessee's likely next governor and possibly a future President of the United States. Lansden was simply in the wrong place at the wrong time—a victim of the unsavory location of his law firm.

H.T. Lansden was also someone of particular importance to me. He had called me the night before and said he had a problem and needed my help. He had not wanted to discuss the details over the phone. I was to have met with him today in his office at 10:00 a.m. Unfortunately, because of his death I may never know what his problem was.... On second thought, maybe I will.

Sarah joined me in the breakfast room. She knows the current and former Mrs. Lansdens. I know Amber, the current wife, who happens to be a member of my Women's Health Club. Sarah would take care of conveying our condolences and would find out the plans regarding a funeral or memorial service. We agreed that she and I would attend the service. We wanted to support the family. H.T. was a good friend, and I was curious. I had an uneasy feeling that his untimely death might be connected to the problem he had wanted to discuss with me.

CHAPTER 2

A Year Ago

Almost a year before Mark Rollins received Lansden's call for help, two men and one woman—all with expensive tastes—sat enjoying a great meal and an exceptional wine at the Metropolitan Grill in Seattle. They were in Seattle on business attending the annual educational conference of the ALA, the Association of Legal Administrators. Their law firms, of course, would not approve of their expensive choice for dinner, but as law firm administrators, each had learned little tricks that kept their out-of-town expenses from being questioned. Thus, while traveling away from their offices and homes, each enjoyed a lifestyle several notches above normal.

They had also learned other tricks, like how to spend their time at a conference playing rather than attending the educational sessions. Depending on the city hosting the event, they spent their days on the golf course or beach, shopping, sightseeing, or sitting by the pool; and in the evenings and late into the night, they dined and caroused. They purchased recordings of the educational sessions, and as they flew home, they listened to those few that would interest their partners. Shortly after returning to work, they prepared and presented written reports on ideas they learned from the conference that would impress their law firm partners. Those reports guaranteed that the firm would continue funding their annual attendance at the ALA conferences.

The three legal administrators (Curtis Ward, Meredith Purcell, and Owen Santo) were buddies even though each lived and worked in different cities. They had been teaming up at the ALA conferences for years. Between conferences, they talked frequently by phone and by e-mail. When one had a problem in his role as law firm administrator, they collaborated, shared experiences and ideas for dealing with the situation.

Each had worked for his law firm for more than ten years. From their point of view, they ran the firms— and their biggest challenge was fending off interference from attorneys who would disrupt their well run offices. According to them, lawyers only get involved in office affairs after attending some legal conference. That is where nationally recognized consultants to the legal profession as well as managing partners from really big law firms tell the audience what they should be doing to run their law firms more like a business.

Lawyers can't stand the idea that their peers might view them as less sophisticated. So when they return from those conferences, they start asking for reports and suggesting things that the three administrators view as just creating more work and complicating their lives. The administrators learned a long time ago how to sidestep those requests. They use the "our-computer-will-not-let-us-do-that" excuse or, if that fails, the "it-will-cost-more-money" ploy. Attorneys are always opposed to adding overhead since it comes directly out of their pockets as partners. Money trumps peer pressure!

The three were finishing dessert when Meredith spoke up, "Okay, whose time is it to pick up the tab?" The other two laughed and pointed at her in unison. "Okay, okay, I knew it was my turn; I was hoping one of you wouldn't remember so I could hang this on him."

Curtis spoke up, "We never forget to spread the damage. That keeps any one of us from going so far over the line that the firm catches on to our *little tricks* for getting the firm to pay for our recreational outings."

Meredith continued, "You know, I don't think we have ever shared our *little tricks*. Curtis, what is yours? How do you manage to get your expenses past the partners at your firm?"

"It's in my pocket." Curtis took out his billfold and passed around an American Express® card. "Our managing partner, Marion W. McTate, Esq., is too important to pay his own American Express bills. He has me do it for him. I review his charges and code the items for payment. Expenses related to a case or a matter get coded to the billing system so that we get reimbursement from the client. All the other items get lumped into our marketing costs as travel and entertainment related to new client development and retention. When I process accounts payable on the 15th and 25th of the month, no one ever questions payment of the managing partner's credit card. That is *verboten!*"

Owen held up the credit card Curtis had passed around. "I don't understand. This card has your name on it just like my own American Express card, so what's the big deal? How does Marion McTate's large standard-lawyer ego fit in?"

Curtis grinned, obviously proud of his con, and explained, "Ah, you see, American Express lets a cardholder add others to their account—you know, like a spouse or a child. I went online to American Express' Web site, signed on as McTate himself, and requested that I, Curtis Ward, be added to the account. Even though the card has my name on it, anything I charge on that card goes on McTate's American Express bill—and I'm the only one that ever looks at his bill. As I said, when I process payment of the charges, no one has the guts to question payment. It's perfect! So guys, what's in *your* wallets?"

They all laughed.

Curtis said, "Okay Meredith, I told you my *little trick*. What is your secret? How are you going to get tonight's bill past the watchdogs in your firm?"

"It's simple. I'm a girl—a nice looking one at that. Some of the partners who have gotten a little too close over the years are scared of me. The other partners trust me. I started working there as a teenager. You know how partners are. They don't want to be bothered with the "bookkeeping" so I can sign checks up to $10,000. And I am the *only* person who checks expense reports— including my own. The managing partner does get a travel and entertainment report every month, but I prepare it. All he wants on it is non-client expenses. If it is billed to clients, he couldn't care less. So, except for the basic travel expenses, like airfare, hotel, etc., I simply 'mistakenly' code things like tonight's dinner to some big client case. Therefore, I don't have to put it on the monthly report."

Curtis interrupted her, "But what about the billing attorney for that client? What happens when they get the draft bill with your expenses on it?"

"Ah, but they don't. I write off the expenses before I print the draft bills. They just kind of disappear mixed in with all of those other write-ups and write-downs. I remember hearing a consultant from Altman Weil talk about law firm write-offs before the client is even billed. He referred to those write-offs as *invisible expenses,* and I promise you, they sure are! That's my secret. Okay, it's your turn, Owen."

Owen didn't answer immediately. His hesitation caused Meredith to say, "Come on, Owen, you can't hold out on us now."

"Guys, I don't like this. It's kind of like premeditation. You guys just confessed that you know exactly what you are doing and that you know it's wrong. I think you both should tell me that you just were pulling my leg with your stories. Let's forget this conversation. As far as I'm concerned, it never happened. That is what both of you should do also—forget this conversation ever took place."

Owen's cohorts stared at him with a sense of surprise. Meredith broke the silence. "Owen, you are full of shit. You just don't want us to know how you work your magic. That probably means you are somebody's bitch or something. I don't give a damn. Let's just get out of this place and go have some fun. What do you say? How about the TWILIGHT? We will increase the average age of the joint, but you guys can chase the young chicks. *Unless that's not your thing, Owen dear!* I can let the young studs chase me. For some reason, the 18 to 20-year-old guys think scoring with we *mature* ladies is their rite of passage to manhood. You guys have a different problem. You have to have star power or money to get the young ladies' attention—so get your cash ready, boys—and Curtis, pull off that damn wedding ring."

Owen smiled at Meredith and said, "I got the star power, babe. Curtis is the one that will have to flash the cash!"

Meredith was at her sarcastic best, "Yeah right, you look like you just walked out of a rodeo or something with your big-ass belt buckle, tight jeans, and fancy-dancy boots."

"Piss off, bitch."

She smiled back and teasingly said, "Good girls get to go to heaven; bad girls get to go everywhere else!"

"They are Luccheses."

"What is?"

"The boots."

"And that's going to get you the chicks?"

"They're all groupies at heart. You forget; I'm from Music City USA."

"Whatever! Come on stud muffins. There is fun to be had, and the night is young."

Curtis pocketed his ring. They left the Metropolitan Grill, still friends and in good spirits.

CHAPTER 3

Sig P232

Because H.T. and I had planned to meet this morning at ten o'clock, I wasn't expected in my office at the WH Club until noon. His senseless death meant I had the morning free. I have to admit to some pent-up anger over the idea of a nameless drunk killing so important a man, so I decided to spend the morning at Uselton's indoor gun range in Franklin checking out my new handgun, a Sig P232.

At the suggestion of Sam Littleton at the FBI, I retired my Taurus PT111 and Cobra C32 Derringer after their use in the Christopher Berry affair which I was instrumental in resolving—an affair well documented in the book *Mark Rollins and the Rainmaker*. When a weapon is fired, it leaves its "fingerprint" on the spent shell casing and bullet fragments. Casings and bullets are collected from a crime scene, stored in evidence rooms, and become part of a national database. Given my occasional off-the-record role with certain government agencies, carrying weapons with a history is not a good idea. Thanks to Sam, both retired handguns have been destroyed in FBI furnaces that make tainted weapons disappear.

The second I had the P232 in my hand, I knew it was the right pistol for me. That's the way it is with a handgun. Either it feels right or it doesn't. The P232 uses .380 ACP cartridges and the magazine holds seven rounds. Three-eighty ammunition is sometimes called a short 9mm since it has the same dimensions as the 9mm but is a smaller cartridge with a relatively short range. Nevertheless, when loaded with personal defense hollow point cartridges, the Sig P232 has plenty of stopping power.

There was another reason the P232 was the right weapon: this isn't the Wild West. Citizens don't strap on their guns and go to town. If you carry, you do so discreetly. As effective as the P232 is, its 17.6 oz. weight puts it in the category of a compact lightweight handgun that is easy to conceal using an inside-the-pants holster or an ankle holster. There are two other concealed carry options that I have started using more often. The 5.11 Tactical Series makes several jackets with concealed carry pockets. I prefer their lightweight station jacket in combination with a pocket holster. The second is a summertime solution I borrowed from the Israeli Secret Service. It is a short sleeve overshirt worn open-front and is long enough to conceal a belt holster. I use a crossdraw holster that keeps the handgun parallel to the ground rather than vertical. The result is a concealed carry that is very difficult for the layperson to detect but provides a quick draw if needed.

There is another important thing about carrying a weapon. If you are doing so because your life, or someone else's life, is in danger then one weapon is not enough. You should always have a backup. My preferred backup is a derringer. You don't sight a derringer as you would a full handgun. You point and fire the derringer. If the target isn't at point-blank range, hitting your bad guy depends on perfect hand-eye coordination. That derringer has to be part of you. That makes selecting the weapon a very personal thing. I haven't found that perfect fit yet. I'm looking for perfection, and I'm determined not to purchase a replacement for the Cobra until I find it.

In the meantime, I have two other handguns that can serve as backup weapons. One is a J-Frame Chief's Special Smith & Wesson .38 from the 1950s. The small snub nose revolver easily disappears under a jacket or shirt. The .38 is a large slow round with plenty of stopping power. Unfortunately, the J-Frame is only a 5-shot revolver. It is a slow reload and ineffective for rapid fire. Like the derringer, it is best used as a backup weapon. The other handgun is a small .22 revolver—quiet and deadly when used correctly, but it lacks the immediacy of mid-body stopping power. It is a black bag weapon not particularly useful in a firefight.

If you ever do need to fire your weapon, that's when the shit will hit the fan! Carrying a weapon means you are prepared to use it and a shooter takes on a lot of responsibility and risk.

The first thing you need to remember as a shooter is that it is *your bullet.* If you fire your weapon at a bad guy and that bullet passes through the target and then hurts or kills some innocent bystander—it is still *your bullet.* You are responsible, financially and legally, for any damage done by *your bullet.*

You want a bullet that flattens or fragments upon impact—a bullet designed to stop the target and not emerge on the other side. That is what personal defense rounds and hollow points are constructed to do. When they strike the bad guy, anywhere, the bullets fragment. The target's nervous system shuts down immediately stopping the opponent with no risk of flow through.

Second, there is only one legal reason to fire your handgun. You or another person must be in imminent fear of death or serious bodily injury. Whether or not that test was met will be decided after the fact by others. I have the advantage of working closely with a number of government agencies who for their own selfish reasons are always around to clean up after me. The ordinary citizen does not have that advantage. If that ordinary citizen fires a weapon at someone, he will pay a price for that action. Even if morally and legally justified, he can expect his picture to be on the front page of local newspapers and he will be the subject of nightly news. He will need a lawyer. It is a cinch that someone is going to sue him. He could have to defend himself in both civil and criminal court.

There is every reason to think carefully before ever carrying a handgun in public. Even in my case, I prefer to leave the pistols at home and limit my weapon to the Swiss Army knife I usually carry—my daughter calls it my "MacGyver" knife. Unfortunately, I live a life where a pocketknife, even one as versatile as my "MacGyver" knife, isn't always adequate protection.

At 8:00 a.m., Tony, my driver, brought Black Beauty around to the front of the house where I was waiting for him, and we left for Uselton's gun range. Black Beauty is the nickname the brain trust guys at the WH Club gave my Lexus after turning it into a high-tech, armored, and armed traveling office.

By 11:00 a.m. I had fired 100 rounds from the Sig and 25 rounds of wad cutter ammo using the snub nose .38— all with 100% kill score. I was firing at paper targets with the waist-up silhouette of a man of average build. The objective is to hit the biggest part of the target—center chest. Headshots are too risky. You want to direct your fire at the portion of the target you are most likely to hit even when your aim is off. Real gunfights are messy. You don't have the luxury of a perfect shot.

With nothing else to do, Tony decided to refresh his shooter skills. He rented a post-war Walther PPK, of James Bond fame, and joined me at the range. Tony is an excellent marksman, but I know from experience that he prefers a baton over a handgun as his weapon of choice. As he has told me many times, the problem with a handgun is that it is deadly force. You are not going to use it unless you are actually under fire. You don't have the same reluctance about using a baton and that makes it the more effective close range offensive weapon. You can render a bad guy completely helpless by breaking his wrist or shattering his kneecap with a single blow—and you don't put innocent bystanders at risk.

We finished up at the range at 11:30 a.m. and headed for the WH Club and my regular weekly management meeting.

CHAPTER 4

The Team

The Women's Health Club is located in the Maryland Farms business campus in the heart of Brentwood, Tennessee. The little community straddles I-65 and starts where the southern edge of Metro Nashville ends. The north side of Old Hickory Blvd. is Nashville and the south side, Brentwood. Brentwood's main street is Franklin Road, which becomes Nashville's Eighth Avenue as you drive into that city. Morning, lunchtime, and five o'clock traffic in Brentwood is a problem.

Fortunately, we made it to the office just ahead of the noonday traffic jam. I didn't have time for lunch before our scheduled weekly management meeting so I called ahead and had Shannon, our receptionist, order me a salmon salad from the Wild Iris. Since we switched our weekly meetings to noon, they have become working lunches. Team members either brown-bagged it or ordered in. When I entered the conference room, the rest of the leadership team was already there.

Meg Scott is the fitness operations manager and my daughter. She is married and has three young children. She is slender, as you would expect, with zero body fat, and one of the very few brunettes you will find around the place. At 5' 8" and 128 pounds, she might not look very imposing, but don't let that fool you. Those 128 pounds are all muscle. Meg is a Black Belt in Taekwondo and is also a proficient kickboxer.

Bryan Gray is the leader of the WH Club brain trust—a small group of loyal computer experts who followed me throughout my business career as a technology entrepreneur. As a result, each member of the brain trust is now a millionaire several times over. What most people don't know is that tucked away inside of the WH Club is a high-tech center with more electronics than most CIA satellite operation centers. Obviously, there is no apparent justification for the technology resources at the Club. Initially, it was just a luxury I could afford to continue even though I was no longer engaged commercially in the technology industry. Today, however, this low visibility operation inside of the Women's Health Club is embarrassingly profitable due to our off-the-record role with various government agencies. Unlike those agencies, we are not subject to Congressional oversight. We don't have to play by the same rules; thus in cyberspace, we can do things and go places they cannot. For that, we get paid the big bucks.

Mariko Lee is Vice President of Security, a role that you will not usually find on the organization chart of other fitness centers. She is a small package. At 5' 2", Mariko just barely qualified for the Marines where she served as a Marine MP. She carries a Beretta Vertec handgun. One of Mariko's problems is concealing the Beretta. Her flamboyant attire doesn't usually leave a lot of places where a gun would go unnoticed. Some people might say she is an exhibitionist. I would describe her as a chameleon who changes her looks and wardrobe to fit the environment she is in or the role she is asked to play. But chameleon or not, she doesn't blend in—ever! She drives a red Aston Martin convertible when she isn't mounted on her big Yamaha Black Max motorcycle. She is also a trust fund baby with an MBA from Vanderbilt's Owen School of Management. She is smart, seductive, and deadly. Her job is to protect people from the danger that seems to follow in my wake. Unfortunately, I have a habit of getting involved in situations that put me and the people around me in harm's way.

Tony Caruso is my driver and personal bodyguard. To do his job, he has to be on top of things at the Club and the family compound. He needs to know what's going on in order to anticipate things, especially things that might involve risk or danger. Tony is an ex-submariner, 5' 10" with the kind of slender build that's required to maneuver in the close quarters of submarine duty. After leaving the Navy, he worked for a private car service. He is an expert behind the wheel with advanced evasion training. I used the car service a couple of times, and after Tony came to

Mariko's aid when she had to defang a couple of tough guys, I talked him into joining my team. He lives at the Rollins family compound—in an apartment over an unattached two-car garage we had built a few years ago.

I looked around the room and quickly surmised that Meg wasn't a happy camper. However, before I gave her the floor, I wanted to alert everyone to Amber Lansden's situation. "Before we get down to business, I want to be sure all of you are aware that Amber's husband, Harold, or H.T. as most people called him, was shot and killed last night. H.T. was a close friend of our family, and Amber is a platinum member of the Club."

"Dad, everyone knows about his death. That and the economy are the only things people were talking about this morning. And you know Amber. She is our resident political type. She collects people. I assume you will handle our social responsibilities—flowers, contribution, or whatever you think is the right thing to do."

"Yes, and Sarah and I plan to attend the service. Obviously, we need to give Amber our support, but I also need to give you guys a heads-up. Before his death, H.T. had called me. All he said was that he had a problem and wanted my help. He didn't want to go into details over the phone so we were to have met today to discuss the matter. His death at the hands of an unknown gunman may have just been a coincidence, but I have a gut feeling that we may find ourselves involved in H.T.'s problem before it is all said and done. So keep your eyes and ears open."

Everyone around the table nodded in agreement. It was time to officially convene our meeting.

CHAPTER 5

Management Meeting

"Okay, let's get the business side of this meeting started. Meg, you're first. You look worried; what's on your mind?"

With a furrowed brow, Meg explained, "Dad, I have never seen our members so worried. It's this economy. The stock market is in the tank. What's even worse is that President Obama has declared war on the very people who pay the taxes to run this country. Companies can't pay contractual bonuses without risking ridicule in the press or being hauled before Congress. They don't dare have their usual sales meetings—meetings that they need to get everyone on the same page for the coming year. They can't reward their top performers with their traditional "100% Club" or achiever events. When Obama talks about redistributing the wealth—it is *their* wealth he wants to *confiscate*. Our members know their taxes are going to soar. Some of them are expecting Obama to go for a wealth tax. It's not economic justice he wants—it's vengeance! He wants to punish the 'haves' and give it back to the 'rightful owners'—what he calls the hard working Americans. That's his agenda—it's to punish the rich. It is like Ayn Rand could see into the future!"

Bryan shook his head and said, "I don't know. We have to do something, don't we?"

Everyone looked at me, wanting my take on things, so I responded. "Bryan is right; we need to do something. But what our new administration is doing is nuts. It isn't entirely their fault, however. Even before Obama was elected, the country had boxed itself in. When you reduce the tax base so that you depend on less than 10% of the population to finance the country, you have created the conditions for a perfect economic storm. When the economy tanks, it is that top 10% whose income dries up.

The guys running the country don't seem to understand that their actions have consequences. Spending has taken a nosedive. Obama has created an environment that puts the lid on compensation and anything that the public might consider extravagant. If people and companies aren't spending, the workers and businesses that depend on those expenditures aren't making any money either. In addition to shutting down spending, they have given corporations the cover to clean house. Today instead of being tainted by mass layoffs, companies get kudos for eliminating thousands of jobs. We are talking about white-collar, gray-collar, and blue-collar jobs. The loss of those jobs sends unemployment payments skyrocketing at the same time tax revenues are falling. It's a vicious cycle—a spiraling down into the depths of an economic valley of despair.

In spite of whatever they say, this is not new territory. We have been through it all before—recessions and credit crunches happen. The housing bubble is just the current iteration of the tulip collapse that happened in the 1600s. This too shall pass.

We know how to get through these things. In fact, I am leaving tomorrow to speak at the ABA Technology Conference in Chicago on the subject of surviving in this downturn. If you do the right things, you can come out of a recession stronger than when you went into it. You need dry powder. That comes from being prudent during the good times. The key is to never over leverage. For law firms, that means leaving some of the earnings in the firm. If they have done that, then they have the dry powder to snare the best people and cherry-pick the most lucrative clients when others are losing them. They have the staying power to hold on to existing clients by sharing their pain with temporary discounts."

Meg interrupted my rant, "We are in the same boat—some of the husbands of our members are dealing with big investment losses, lower compensation, and higher taxes. They are looking for ways to cut spending, and the wife's membership in the WH Club is at the top of the hit list. You have to admit that we kind of fall into that extravagant expenditure category.

I have no idea how to fix this. If I had to guess, I would say that we could lose over 50% of our members in the next few months, and I wouldn't be at all surprised if the losses were even higher. It's just awful, Dad! I don't see what we can do to prevent it."

All eyes were on me again, but it was Mariko who spoke, "Well, Boss, maybe we need to take the advice you are planning to give to law firms at the ABA conference. *Share your client's pain. Reduce your price; give them a temporary discount.*"

"Mariko, I'm thinking along those lines, but a price decrease is not enough. It will not save the day. Membership in the Club would still be discretionary—an unessential luxury. We're too easy a target. What we need to do is to take the WH Club completely out of the picture—off the chopping block."

Meg jerked to attention and asked, "How?"

"It is time to quit burning daylight over this issue. Let's make an announcement today. We waive 100% of our normal monthly membership fee. You can work out the exact wording, but I suggest it go something like the following:

> *Our members represent the top echelon of Nashville's social and economic society. During good times, you are the people who support the unique mission of the exclusive Women's Health Club while also paying most of this country's taxes and funding our charities, colleges, churches, and other good causes. You deserve some payback,*

and we are going to do our share. So during this temporary period of economic crisis, we will waive our monthly membership fee. That means that for all <u>current</u> WH Club members, your membership for the next nine months will be free. You can enjoy the benefits of this exclusive club without concern about spending on what is admittedly a luxury—but it is one you have earned."

"Dad, how can we afford to do that?" Meg gasped.

"I don't see that we really have a choice. You have already said we could lose 50% or more of our fee revenue as long as we remain in the cost-cutting crosshairs of our members' spouses."

Meg sat there slowly shaking her head. "I was thinking we're dead, but in less than a minute, you come up with a solution that wasn't on anyone else's list of options. It seems so simple now, but for all of us, it was an idea completely outside of our reach. Maybe you should run for President of the U.S. next time!"

I laughed with everyone else before saying, "I don't think I would make it through the vetting process, Meg. Besides, the decision to give up our membership fees for nine months isn't as tough as it might sound. Have you seen the projections we are expecting from the Palle tour? *The Journey to Perfection in Mind and Body with Yoga Master Ajay Palle* is turning out to be a blockbuster. We are going to make a bundle. It isn't continuing revenue. It is a one shot deal, but it will more than offset our loss of membership fees for this fiscal year."

Tony who had remained quiet until now said, "What is the Palle thing? I think I'm missing something."

Bryan jumped in to explain, "Tony, a few months ago Meg thought we were going to lose her number one yoga instructor, Tori. Tori wanted to take a sabbatical so she could return to India to refresh her studies under her old Master—one Ajay Palle. The Chief came up with the idea of bringing Palle here versus Tori going to India. The tour was to serve two purposes. First, to offset the cost of transplanting Palle to the states for some period of time and second, the prospects of becoming a rock star would help close the deal with Palle. Like most people, he wanted his fifteen minutes of fame. The Chief put Mrs. Rollins on the project from a marketing standpoint, and now it looks like his idea is going to do a lot more than just break even—it's going to make millions."

I nodded in agreement. "Bryan has it right. Unless we spend it, the folks at Goldman are just going to get more money from us that they have to find a safe place to park, and that is getting harder. So why not give our members a break and use some of it to head off membership losses?" I looked at my watch, and it was a little before four o'clock in the evening so I said, "Unless anyone has a pressing issue, I am going to adjourn until next week." I looked around the room and no one indicated a need to extend the meeting. I said, "Meeting adjourned."

I headed downstairs to my office to check my e-mail and to go through the decreasing number of snail mail items from those people who still put things on paper. As I went down the central stairs, Shannon, our always-smiling receptionist, was waiting for me.

"Good afternoon, Mr. Rollins! Would you like to make a contribution?" Shannon always has a cause. She enthusiastically tries to save the world.

"What is it this time, Shannon?"

"Well, do you know what Madonna is doing?"

"Madonna the singer?"

"Yes, Mr. Rollins. She is trying to take a baby boy away from his grandmother!"

"You mean the orphan she's adopting?"

"It is *not* an adoption. It's kidnapping! She is *stealing* that little African boy."

"Come on, Shannon; the boy is in an orphanage. He will have a dream life with Madonna. If he stays where he is, he will probably die of some awful disease—from Guinea worms to AIDS."

Shannon started to tear up. I was raining on her parade. She clearly believed in the noble savage image and had a deep-seated belief that it was wrong for some rich person to take the boy out of his natural environment. The truth is it is an awful environment that somehow has to change. No one seems to know how.

I continued, "Look Shannon, you know I always support your causes. I'll write you a check for $1000, but don't be so hard on Madonna. She is trying to do some good. Use my contribution to improve the life of the African orphans that don't get adopted. Okay?"

Shannon's face lit up. "Okay—and thank you, Mr. Rollins; you are always so generous. I hate to keep asking you."

"Don't stop, Shannon; don't ever stop. We need people who care—who want to make a difference. Just don't turn against others who also care—do good, like always."

Shannon gave me a weak smile and asked, "Will you wear this for me today?" She handed me a brown support wristband with the embossed words *Save the Children*.

"Of course I will, Shannon." I slipped it on my wrist and continued to my office.

My snail mail in-box included a nice letter from the Conference Chairperson for the upcoming annual educational conference of the Association of Legal Administrators. Apparently my Seattle presentation last year on the Business of Legal Services received high marks from the attendees so they wanted me back for this year's conference in Dallas. The suggested topic for my proposed presentation was Guarding Against Embezzlement in the Law Firm. Her letter included an e-mail address so I quickly typed my acceptance, thanked her for the nice words, and updated my calendar.

Other than e-mails asking for political contributions, there wasn't much else in my in-box. I deleted them and was happy to head for home. Sarah and I had been invited by friends to join them at a local champagne tasting.

Before I left for home, I retrieved an American flag lapel pin I wore after the 9/11 terror attack on the World Trade Center. I hadn't worn the pin for some time. I put it on. But this time I put it on upside down—an upside down national flag was at one time an internationally recognized distress signal.

CHAPTER 6

"Ding Dong"

"Mr. Nelson, I just learned about Lansden!" shouted Gordon Seemann.

"Yeah, the 'great litigator' is dead. Makes you want to sing, doesn't it?" The man laughed and began chanting, "Ding Dong! The old barrister is dead. Which old barrister? The Wicked Barrister! Ding Dong! The Wicked Barrister is dead." At the end of his out-of-tune ditty, he asked, "Has a nice ring to it, doesn't it?"

"Mr. Nelson, the man is dead! Aren't we being a little too flippant about it?" Seemann wondered if Nelson had gone over the edge.

Keith Nelson was fifty-eight. He was a big man, seated behind a big desk in a big office. He had worked on Wall Street most of his life. Million dollar bonuses had been amassed into an even bigger fortune. He needed that fortune to support his lifestyle. Now, with a new wife and just when he was beginning to enjoy that wealth, it was all at risk—at risk because of that stubborn-ass country lawyer, Lansden, out to make a name for himself.

When the housing boom really started taking off, Nelson was smart enough to see the mortgage refinancing opportunity. With interest rates on the decline and home values skyrocketing, the new generation of homeowners had discovered they could turn their homes into an ATM machine. They could get ready cash to pay down credit cards or other bills just by refinancing. So what if that meant higher mortgage payments? They could just run up the credit cards again and in a couple of years do another refi. Nelson saw that he could pocket big fees by handling the paperwork and passing the risk on to others.

He left the investment firm and started his own mortgage company, Hudson Bluff Mortgage, Inc. The system was rigged, and he saw that it was a game you could not lose. He used to say, "I don't take the risk, just the profits." Get him talking, and he would let you know how it is done. "You close a refi deal. You sell that paper to some dumb-as-hell bureaucrat. You take that money and make more deals. You just do it over and over again. That is all we do—turn the money and take the profits. The bureaucrats bundle the mortgages into $100 million packages that the people on Wall Street are all too happy to sell—for a fee—to institutional and fund investors all over the world. Then the money flows back into the mortgage refi market. It is just one big recycling of money.

Everyone is happy. Everyone is making money." ... "That was until the shit hit the fan," he later said.

"Gordon, you don't understand! You should be celebrating. Your butt has just been pulled out of the fire. That bastard, Lansden, had us by the balls over the Fenio mortgage case. Hell, Fenio hocked his house to start a bunch of taco stands—refinanced their place for a hell of a lot more than it was worth. He didn't even have a job. Lost his shirt—and, when the bank was foreclosing, Fenio's wife goes running to the Great Harold T. Lansden claiming we shouldn't have loaned the damn money! We are supposed to have told Fenio it was okay to lie like shit on the application. Lansden was going to sue us for the big bucks!

To hell with the money—after he got through with the two of us, I figured we would be damn lucky to stay out of jail. Hell, we were both going to be ruined by that hillbilly. I'm the CEO; you're the CFO. We are the people the public wants to see swinging from a lamppost. We are the 'corporate fat cats'. Obama, that damn Congress, and the fucking news media has whipped our dumb-as-a-post citizens into a pitchfork marching mob. This time they aren't after Frankenstein—they want a piece of *you* and *me*. They want to stick those pitchforks into some mean, bad corporate executives!"

Gordon Seemann was a young CPA. He joined the staff of a large national CPA firm right out of college. Three years later,he was the senior member of the audit team assigned to the Hudson Bluff Mortgage, Inc. account. It was Seemann's job to review the accounting firm's proposed management letter with Mr. Nelson before issuing the final report to the Board of Directors. The initial draft had been strongly critical of a number of practices followed by the company. Mr. Nelson got the young CPA to drop some and soften other recommendations. Two months after completion of the audit, Gordon Seemann joined the mortgage company as its Chief Financial Officer.

"Mr. Nelson, I don't understand what we are supposed to have done that was so bad. We have 6,000 employees and 4,000 agents and independents. We can't know what every one of those is doing all the time. How can they make us responsible for a few over-enthusiastic sales types who went overboard?"

"Gordon, we are the worst kind of bad guys—fat cats with big salaries. Lansden would have convinced the jury that we deliberately set out to rip off old people, widows, and orphans. You and I know it wasn't that way. Right? Everyone was supposed to be working off the same forms. Everyone was using 'stated income' so we could commit on the spot. If we hadn't gone along with it, we wouldn't have had any business. The competition didn't give us time to verify the income information. Like everybody else—we let the applicants fill in their income information on the application form. We take their word for it. The applicants swear to it. What are we supposed to do, call our customers liars and crooks?

We had some bad apples like everyone else. Our jerk agent in that hick-town Nashville was one of them. Okay, so he told people what to put on the forms. They say he recruited refis—showed people how they could get some real spending money by borrowing more than their house was worth. Damn fools took the money and blew it— big ass vacations, gambling, or whatever. Hell, they just pissed it away! Then the buffoons could not afford the damn payments. And, that is supposed be *our* fault? How were we supposed to know that? Hell, we were, what, 1500 miles away in New York? We gave them the damn book. We told them to follow the damn thing. What the hell did they think we wrote those procedures for? We depend on people to follow our rules, right? If they don't, if they do bad things, then *they* are the jerks who should be hauled to court—sent to jail. Not us!"

"Mr. Nelson, Nashville wasn't the only place. A lot of that stuff was going on in Orange County, right? So why is Nashville such a big problem?"

"Gordon, the problem wasn't about Nashville. It was about that dead bastard, Lansden. He wasn't just some lawyer. He was a damn politician. That guy was trying to make a national name for himself. Hell, the man actually thought he could be the *President*. We are taking care of those Orange County problems. We're doing it quietly. That damn Lansden wasn't into doing things quietly. Nashville could have snowballed and taken us down. Lansden wanted blood—ours!

It is different now. The 'great litigator' is dead—no more gravy train for the other partners in his law firm. Lansden's firm is going to have their hands full trying to fill his shoes. Hell, they can't do it! H.T. Lansden was a busy man—had a zillion balls in the air. With Lansden out of the picture, we can head this thing off before it does snowball, or worse, lead to a class action suit. We need to get to the client and settle—and get them to sign a non-disclosure agreement. We make them an offer they can't refuse, but one we can afford."

"I wish I shared your optimism, Mr. Nelson. The law firm may not roll over on this. What if they want to hold out for a mega jury verdict?"

"They don't have any reason to go big time with this. It was Lansden's ambition that was driving this thing. They are smarter than that. They know how long a court case would take. We would appeal. If we slow-walked things, it would be years before the client or the law firm would see one damn penny. Hell, the publicity would destroy us anyway, and their jury award would be worthless. Lansden didn't give a shit about the money. A settlement will immediately put money in the firm's bank account. It will be one less of Lansden's hot potatoes that the firm has to deal with. And Lansden's death may have them worrying about their own hides. The timing is right. It always pays to take advantage of someone else's misery."

"Anything I can do to help, Mr. Nelson?"

"Gordon, it wouldn't hurt to have a friend inside Lansden's law firm—someone who keeps us posted— maybe even in a position to encourage the Fenios to accept the settlement."

"We may have an inside man—someone we have been cultivating, just in case. He contacted us about a job—a big salary position in our legal department, Assistant General

Counsel. He hinted that he might be able to help us out with the Fenio case. I've been stringing him along."

"Who is it?"

"His name is Bill Maxwell."

"How far down the ladder is he?"

"He claims he is one of three senior associates they have talked to about moving to partner level."

Nelson expressed his skepticism, "Wouldn't that kind of make our job less attractive to him?"

"The firm has a funny compensation system. I won't bore you with the details, but according to Maxwell the only thing being a partner gets you in that firm is personal liability for the firm's debt and for malpractice claims."

"See what you can get out of him. Who is going to take over the Fenio case? Is there any chance he can get involved through his end—help us get this thing settled ASAP? You can tell him it would make the Assistant General Counsel job his. Hell, tell him it will be Vice President and Assistant General Counsel."

"Will do."

"Yep, Gordon, you should celebrate. It is a good day. The Wicked Barrister is dead, or maybe I should say the Bastard is dead—and good riddance to him!"

"Mr. Nelson, you seem a little too happy about this."

"You bet your ass, I'm happy!"

"I mean, we didn't have anything to do with this, did we?"

Keith Nelson laughed. "Why Gordon, how can you ask such a thing? I'm just the Good Bastard whose house fell on the Bad Bastard. It was an act of God." He looked up at the ceiling, raised his hands, and laughed as he exclaimed, "Thank you, God!"

Then Nelson stopped laughing and focused on Seemann. "And you should thank God too, Gordon. If Lansden had had his way, your stock options would be worthless. You would be out of a job—*penniless*. The only job you could get is as a shoe salesman, or worse, a mattress salesman. Jail might have even looked good to you—a roof over your head and three squares a day. Count your blessings, my son, and don't question good fortune when it comes your way. Just keep thinking—*Ding Dong! The Wicked Barrister is dead!*"

CHAPTER 7

Chicago

I woke up at 5:00 a.m. as usual. Before the days of Dorin and Gabriela, I usually worked in my sunroom office until 6:30 or 7:00 a.m. That is when the smell of coffee told me that Sarah was up. I really valued those couple of hours when the house was completely still. That was my creative time. Unfortunately, the negative side of having Dorin and Gabriela is the loss of a good portion of my alone time. Their routine included rising at 5:30 a.m. That ended my quiet time. I would continue to work, but not as productively, until exactly 6:30 a.m. That's when Gabriela served breakfast. If either Sarah or I were late, she would pout for the rest of the day. After one or two such episodes, neither Sarah nor I were willing to pay that price again so we have given in and cater to her time schedules.

We sat down to silver-dollar-size pancakes and link sausages. That meant it was Tuesday. Another Gabriela trait was a menu unwaveringly attached to the days of the week. Sarah may have made concessions for Gabriela's quirks, but she wasn't about to relinquish total control of her kitchen. She had insisted on lower calorie versions of the sausage—gourmet Smoked Chicken & Apple. Sarah had also ruled that the breakfast menu always include a fruit dish. This morning it was fresh yogurt and peach slices. The pancakes and AAA maple syrup was delicious, but I had the plane flight to Chicago ahead of me and didn't need a heavy breakfast. I sampled the main course and went for the yogurt with gusto.

Sarah got to the morning *Tennessean* first. The obituary was a long one. H.T. had a distinguished career. He was an important part of the Nashville community. In lieu of flowers, the family asked that donations be made to Tennessee's Crime Victims Fund. The funeral was to be a private family affair. However, a memorial service open to the public was scheduled for this coming Friday at 10:30 a.m. in the Ryman Auditorium, the original home of Nashville's Grand Ole Opry. We made our plans to attend.

Because of absurd estate tax laws, Sarah and I maintain separate cash and investment accounts which we have each had placed in revocable trusts. She and I each wrote $2,500.00 checks. I left mine with Sarah to mail with hers.

I'm on the faculty of the ABA Technology Conference. I spent the next three days in Chicago. It is a great city with some of my favorite restaurants, including Charlie Trotter's. I didn't make it to Charlie's on this trip, however. Tuesday night I had dinner with a good friend from the Themis Software days, Linda Cunningham. She is a real meat-and-potatoes lady so we went to the Capital Grille. Like The Palm, Smith & Wollensky, and Morton's, the Capital Grille has evolved into a chain. Nevertheless, it is one of the best steak houses, bar none.

The Capital Grille's service is a class act. You will not be overwhelmed by a large wait staff, but I promise you that your server will be a seasoned professional who seemingly has only your table to worry about. Ours was a young lady, Christen Matous. I ordered a bottle of Cheval Blanc 1996. Although it was not technically bad, it was certainly disappointing. The 1996 has a reputation for being one of the great Bordeaux's lighter vintages, but this particular bottle was lifeless—dead with no character and little nose. Christen asked to taste the wine. She sampled it, agreed with the verdict, immediately took the guilty bottle away, and removed it from our bill. I replaced it with a wonderful bottle of Silver Oak from the Alexander Valley.

The next night was a return to one of my regular haunts—Harry Caray's. While the food at Harry Caray's is probably not going to win any culinary awards, the atmosphere combines with good and consistent dishes to make it a great choice for dinner. I'm a creature of habit and always order the same thing—lamb chops oregano. I have never had better.

My presentation on *Surviving in This Economic Downturn* was on the last day of the conference. Comparisons to the

Great Depression in the media fanned by an administration determined not to let a "crisis go to waste" has everyone running scared. The questions on everyone's minds are: how bad is it going to get? and can I survive? I tried to add some reality to counter the hype. We will come out of this downturn just as we have come out of others many times in the past. There will be winners and losers, of course. The winners will be law firms in a position to capitalize on the opportunities created by economic turmoil. They are the firms that exercised prudence during the good times. Most businesses respond to a recession in the same way. They curtail investments in new or replacement assets. They shut down advertising expenditures, stop all non-essential travel, impose a hiring freeze, and eliminate or reduce salary increases. Thus, most businesses sacrifice momentum during such times. The prudent firm will have the dry powder needed to buck the herd mentality. They will have the capacity to take advantage of investment opportunities, hire while others are shrinking, and aggressively add market share while others are losing it.

My advice to law firm managing partners attending my session was first, don't follow the pack and shut down. Instead, pull your team together and start thinking ahead. What new risks are we facing and what can we do to minimize them? What new opportunities will present themselves and how can we capitalize on them? You must plan, set objectives, measure performance, and hold people accountable for a new environment. It isn't business as usual; it is a different game, and you need a different game plan. Second, do take steps to assure that you have adequate capital—speed up billing, shorten collection cycles, increase requirements for front-end payments and client advances, reduce funding of client expenses, and keep more margin dollars in the firm (hold back more profits).

An hour and a half in front of a couple hundred attorneys followed by another thirty minutes of one-on-one conversations with attendees who keep you at the podium leaves you a little limp. I was already experiencing the *fourth-day syndrome.* I have often been asked what I don't like about traveling. My answer is the fourth day. That is when the wear and tear of traveling has taken its toll, and you would rather be home.

On this trip the "fourth-day syndrome" came a day early. The next best thing to being at home is a good old-fashioned hamburger. So for lunch, I skipped the fancy restaurants and headed for the bridge near the Tribune Tower and Wrigley Building and took the stairs that go under the bridge to the out-of-the-way home of an American original—the Billy Goat Tavern made famous by John Belushi's Saturday Night Live sketch: "Cheezborger! Cheezborger! No fries, cheeps! No Pepsi, Coke!"

* * *

While the ABA conference was uneventful, my airport experience was not. I was flying Southwest out of Midway. I ran into Bob Adams who was traveling back to

Nashville on the same flight. Bob is the managing partner of a small Nashville law firm located on Second Avenue about three blocks from Lansden, Tillman and Hall. He brought up the H.T. subject and we both expressed our admiration for the man. What got my attention was his statement that he had heard from a friend in the police department that investigators may not be so sure about the random shooting thing. As he put it, "They think the newspapers were too quick to label this simply a case of being in the wrong place at the wrong time."

For the remainder of the flight, Bob's words kept running through my head. H.T.'s death could not have been simply a case of being in the wrong place at the wrong time!

I landed in Nashville about 8:30 p.m. Spot Parking Service brought the Lexus around to the baggage area and I headed home. As I pulled onto the interstate, I called Bryan. He answered after the second ring.

"What's up, Chief?"

"Bryan, do you still have an inside track to Nashville's CSI team?"

"I don't, but Big John does. You remember; he worked there before I recruited him for our team back in the Themis days. What do you need?"

"Find out what you can about the Harold T. Lansden case. Do the police still think this was just a random shooting and if not, why not? And who are they looking at as possible suspects and why, etc. etc. etc.?"

"Okay, I'm on it."

"Thanks, Bryan. I'm back in Nashville but will be attending H.T.'s memorial service tomorrow. If I make it into the Club, it will be late in the day. Don't wait for me; have Big John call me when he has some answers."

"Roger that, Chief."

When I finally made it home, Dorin and Gabriela had already retired to their upstairs apartment. It felt like old times—the time before we came under the thumb of domestics. Sarah offered to cook me an omelet. I had grabbed a bite, a Chicago-style dog, at Midway so I wasn't hungry. Instead, I fixed a Skyy Martini, cold and dry, and poured a Bailey's for Sarah. We dimmed the lights, turned on the TV, and watched the Monday night episode of *24* that we had recorded. It was good to be home.

CHAPTER 8

Memorial Service

I don't like funerals so I was happy that H.T.'s was a private affair. However, the memorial service at the Ryman Auditorium was anything but private. Tony drove Sarah and me to the Ryman so we wouldn't have to deal with parking—which was a good thing because there wasn't any. The Ryman was already standing room only; yet, there was a line of people still trying to get in. The line wrapped around the corner at Third and Broadway ending at the door to Tootsies Orchid Lounge. That wasn't a coincidence. Those who would have added to the length of the line had succumbed to the temptation and were inside Tootsies drinking a cold one and listening to country music.

Fortunately, we knew somebody and didn't have to deal with the line. Tony let us out at the old stage door.

We had reserved seats down front, center stage, in section four. First, however, we were ushered backstage to express our condolences to the family before the start of the service.

The presence of H.T.'s current wife, Amber, and his former wife, Cassie, at the service made the visitation strained and uncomfortable. Amber had been H.T.'s secretary before he and Cassie divorced. The idea of a home wife and business wife doesn't really fit well with the home wife. Amber and H.T.'s relationship during his first marriage may have been purely platonic but, according to Sarah, you will never convince Cassie. In her mind, Amber was a home wrecker, a social climber out to snare her husband for his money and country club connections. Unlike Cassie, who didn't care for the limelight, Amber took the job of being Mrs. Lansden as a mission to advance the couple's social and political position. If there was an important charity event in Nashville, Amber was chair, co-chair, or a major sponsor. She struck me as a needy person who was always seeking approval. She gathered people around her. But make no mistake—she was the queen, and they were just her loving court.

We spoke quietly to Cassie and her son and daughter. Both of the children were now adults with successful careers. Then Sarah and I moved on to Amber who was already surrounded by her attendants. I was surprised by her demeanor. She was smiling and outgoing, playing the crowd of well-wishers as a happy hostess might have. Where were the tears? Maybe she had already shed them. But I couldn't help feeling that she was enjoying the attention way too much. There seemed to be an indifference or a disconnect about the reason we were all here. As we spoke to her, she never once referred to H.T. or reflected on his life. There was no confirmation of his existence—no comment that he was loved, that he did so much good, that he wanted to help people. There was none of that. Maybe it just hadn't sunk in yet. Maybe that was it—maybe not. Whatever the reason, it bothered me. I had hoped to get Amber aside to speak to her privately but she was too quick to dismiss Sarah and me so she could greet the next well-wisher, the Mayor.

H.T. was a good man, and good men do not memorialize quickly. The list of those eulogizing the man was impressive enough to bring out the Secret Service. A host of Nashville's stars contributed their time to give H.T. a true Nashville send-off. The Ryman is often referred to as the Mother Church of Country Music so the performances were quite appropriate. *Amazing Grace, Freebird, Broken Wings, Peace in the Valley, You'll Never Walk Alone, One Day at a Time,* and the *Circle of Life,* each sung by a different artist, were woven among the eulogies. If by the end of the service you still had a dry eye, the last performer would have done it for you. It was Faith Hill dressed in all black singing *There You'll Be* as the grieving widow, Amber, released a single white dove.

H.T. was not only a prominent political figure on the state and national scene; he was a hero to many underprivileged people. He didn't just talk the talk. He would roll up his sleeves and help others. He was always on the right side of the issues. While he was a high-priced attorney, he was never reluctant to handle a case *pro bono* when he thought justice and fairness deserved his attention. He also was not intimidated by those who considered themselves above the law. He teamed up with Fred Thompson years ago to expose corruption involving the sale of pardons that led to the removal of a sitting Governor of Tennessee.

One group you would think any lawyer would be reluctant to challenge is the sitting judges. But when Tennessee's Democratic legislature cooked up a scheme to replace the election of our judges with gubernatorial appointments, H.T. sued the state. That battle is still going on in the courts and unless there is someone else out there with the courage to pick up the mantle and fight the establishment, it may well die for lack of a leader.

There is always the question of what drives a man like my friend H.T. It isn't money, although he knew how to use it well. It isn't power as such. It isn't trophies. It is fans—followers—like an actor or an actress who thrives on the sound of applause, H.T., like his wife, needed people. The difference is that H.T. liked people. Amber just collected them.

It was that need for people that led to the divorce from his first wife and H.T.'s closest brush with a scandal. Cassie Lansden was embarrassed by attention. She didn't like it and increasingly tried to avoid the limelight—the same light that H.T. craved. When the divorce came, people thought H.T. was dumping Cassie for a trophy wife. Amber was a little younger and attractive though she was not beautiful. But she had what Cassie didn't have—stage presence. She thrived on attention. I think to Amber, H.T. was a way to put a star on her dressing room door. Even when Cassie and H.T. were still married, Amber was at H.T.'s side during public events. While Cassie stayed home, Amber and H.T. were always together—pressing the flesh and waving the flag. People who didn't know H.T. well began to think of *them* as a couple. In the end, the divorce boiled down to the fact that H.T. just couldn't live the kind of life that Cassie wanted, and Cassie detested his.

The service ended around 1:00 p.m. but no one seemed ready to leave. People stood around talking about the man we had lost—what he had done and what he might have done. I looked for Amber, but she was nowhere to be found.

Tony picked us up. I suggested lunch for the three of us at the Hermitage Hotel. The Hermitage is one of the last grand hotels of its vintage, circa 1910. It is in the shadow of Tennessee's capitol, and the basement restaurant used to be a men's-only club. It was a power center where deals and laws were made.

After we had taken our table and ordered lunch, I asked, "Tony, have you been here before?"

"No, Mr. R., I haven't. It's a nice place. Pretty impressive. I feel like I've gone back in time about a hundred years."

"Tony, this grand old hotel had become a derelict in pretty bad shape before a group of investors completely restored it. Saving historic properties was one of the Carter administration's priorities. The President backed that up with tax incentives—and they worked. Many vintage properties are still around today as a result. If you are a trivia person, there's a lot of it associated with this hotel. For example, Minnesota Fats made the Hermitage his home after the renovation. He used to keep a private pool table on the mezzanine where he would entertain guests and sell them his autograph. But I want you to check out the men's room before I tell you one of the hotel's more recent claims to fame."

Tony gave me an odd look before he finally said, "If you say so. Which way?"

I pointed. Tony left the table and sauntered in the direction I had pointed.

After Tony left, I asked, "Sarah, did you think Amber's behavior was a little strange?"

"Well, it wasn't what I was expecting. Visits with the family are never easy for me, especially when they are visibly suffering from their loss. So in a way, it was a relief. It's hard to know how you would react in similar circumstances."

"I know, Sarah, but all I saw was a happy hostess entertaining her guests."

"Mark, in her defense she has had a lot of practice as a hostess. She knows how to be a good one. She doesn't know how to be a widow yet. She just buried, or in this case cremated, a husband. She is doing what she knows how to do—put on a brave face—smile, and wave."

"At the same time, Sarah, a good hostess makes you feel like you are the only person in the room. It was as if the event was all about her and not about H.T."

"Well, the truth be told, funerals and memorial services are for the living. The dead don't care."

"*Touché*, my loved one!"

"Besides Mark, women notice things about other women that you guys look right past. She was well made up, but I know her better than you do. She looked stressed to me, and even perfect makeup couldn't completely hide her pallor and puffy eyes."

"Maybe you're right. Maybe I'm being too hard on her. I wonder what kind of shape Amber is in financially. Law firms usually don't continue compensation payments to the spouse of a deceased partner. I'm sure H.T. was drawing a lot of money out of the firm and that is going to stop now. He and Amber were never reluctant to spend money. He was still young, and most young upwardly mobile men do not have much put away for a rainy day."

"I don't know, Mark. Amber was just a secretary before she married H.T. so she wouldn't have money of her own to fall back on. They lived an upscale life, and I'm sure they do have very high expenses that will not go away easily—mortgage on that big Belle Meade place—*plus* the house in Breckenridge, the apartment in New York, and various club memberships—not to mention the divorce settlement and H.T.'s alimony payments."

"How do you know so much, Sarah?"

"Ladies like to talk about other ladies, my dear."

Tony returned to our table with a smile. I asked, "Well, Tony, what do you think?"

"I think that's the nicest john I've ever seen! In the hotel's heyday, I'm sure there were white jacketed attendants standing by to hand you a towel, brush off your jacket, and probably even shine your shoes."

"You nailed it, Tony. It is very period correct—art deco, black and green tile, and matching marble. Here is the trivia fact for you: That men's room is the recipient of *America's Best Restroom* award."

Tony laughed appreciatively. He and I discussed some of the room's details while Sarah threatened to go look at it. The server brought our lunch and the conversation paused in honor of the attractively presented and delicious fare.

* * *

It was almost 3:00 p.m. when Tony had us en route back home. Thanks to the brain trust, my Lexus is a high-tech mobile office. I turned on the rear display to check my e-mail. The message from Big John that I was hoping for was there:

> *Per Bryan's request, I contacted friends at CSI for the purpose of determining where the authorities are in regard to the death of Harold T. Lansden. Lansden was killed by a single .25 caliber shot to the head. Call for more details.*

I by-passed the voice command capability and opted for John's speed dial number instead.

Big John answered his phone quickly, "Thanks for calling, Mr. Rollins."

"John, I am a little surprised about the .25 caliber ammo."

"You're not alone, Mr. Rollins. According to the people at CSI, that is what first brought the random shooting story into question. A .25 caliber gun is not what you expect to find on the street or in the hands of a drunken guy shooting up the place. It is a woman's lightweight gun, strictly high society, something they put in their purses along with mad money. It's a close range weapon and even then is a poor handgun for personal defense. If a guy gets a little too aggressive, it has some scare power but very little else."

"I certainly can't argue with any of that, John, but you said it was the first thing that made them suspicious. What else is there?"

"They didn't find any spent cartridge shells at the scene, nor did they find the business end of the .25 ammo other than the single round in the lawyer's brain."

"Aha!—I see the problem! If they didn't find any shells, the drunken shooter must have been using a revolver. An automatic would have ejected the shells as new rounds were loaded into the chamber. A revolver would have retained the shells until manually ejected. But, of course, there is no such thing as a .25 revolver! One was never made. So there must have been *two* handguns and *two* shooters—the drunk and the person who actually shot H.T."

"Bingo! And the witnesses all mentioned the drunk's gun had a bright barrel flash and a loud report. That doesn't sound like a .25 pop gun. On top of that, the witnesses say the shooter was firing in the air. Lansden, who you would think would be looking at the shooter like everyone else, was shot in the *side* of his head—not the front as you would have expected. Here's another kicker: the coroner's autopsy indicated contaminants in the wound track. The CSI people speculate that the bullet passed through some foreign material before entering Lansden."

"What kind of material?" I asked.

"They don't know yet. The amounts are microscopic. It will take some time before they are likely to narrow it down."

"What do they think the material means?"

Big John replied, "Maybe the person who shot Lansden needed to conceal the weapon from him. That would imply Lansden knew his killer. You know, they could have been walking together, talking to each other. The killer fired the gun from its hiding place—a purse or jacket pocket. That would account for at least one of the missing shell casings—the one from the gun that actually killed your friend. The casing would have been ejected into the concealment device. The killer could also have used the device, the purse or jacket, to avoid powder burns that would have told us it was a close-range shot—too close to have come from the drunk's gun."

"What about powder burns?"

"There were trace amounts. Not much, but enough not to be consistent with the reported distance between our drunken shooter and the victim."

"John, where are the investigators going with all this?"

"Lansden was a friend of the department and a big supporter of the Fraternal Order of Police. They feel like he was one of their own. They are not going to let this go cold. But they are keeping what they know quiet and plan to stay covert with the investigation as long as they can. Right now, the public accepts the random violence thing, so they aren't going to rock the boat until they establish a high probability suspect or as they say now, a 'person of interest'."

"John, isn't it more likely to be *persons* of interest? I mean, there must have been more than one person involved."

"I agree. And here is another problem with the drunken shooter scenario. Where did he go? He was supposed to be blind drunk! This is a prime tourist area. Cops were all over the place in seconds. They had the place cordoned off and shut down in less than a minute—and yet, they didn't come up with our drunk. How did he get away so quickly—car, motorcycle, or what? Even if he had access, he should have been too drunk to drive! The drunk thing could have been an act. They could have ducked into a building, maybe even into the law firm, and become just another sober citizen concerned with the lawlessness of the area."

"Sounds logical. Who is the lead detective?"

"Parker McGovern. He's an older guy close to retirement but as savvy as they come."

"It couldn't hurt for me to contact this Parker McGovern. Can you get me his contact info?"

"Sure thing. I'll e-mail it to you."

"Thanks, John."

"Will do, Mr. Rollins. Have a nice weekend."

"Thank you; and by the way—good job!" I ended the connection.

Sarah had been listening and now said, "It is very hard for me to believe someone would intentionally kill H.T."

"Yeah, I'm with you on that count. But I will say that if he did meet his end due to evil, and it is certainly beginning to look that way, I'm going to make sure the bad guys are brought to justice. However for now, my dear sweet wife, I'm going to put the Lansdens' affair out of my mind. I promise you, this weekend is going to be family time."

Sarah smiled and said sarcastically, "Right!"

CHAPTER 9

Phone Conversation

"I think you need to get out of town for a while!" The way he said it made it clear that the subject was not up for debate.

"Why?" she pleaded.

"People are curious about H.T. They are going to be asking questions—trying to put some meaning into his death."

"So?" There was defiance in her question but not the resolve to stand up to him.

"Just pack up and go," he said abruptly. Then his tone softened, "Go to Aspen, or even better, go to that place in Provence that you like."

"I don't see why," she resisted. "There are a lot of things...."

"Look, I can take care of what needs to be done. There is too much for *me*—and you—to lose if you get careless." He tried to restrain his irritation.

"I'm not going to say anything that I shouldn't."

"You don't know that. Reporters could start digging into things. Just listen to me and play it safe—let things cool down."

"How do I explain my going away so soon?"

"Just say that you had to get away from it all ... to try to put your life back together."

"What about your wife?"

"I promise I'll make that happen, but not now! We *have* to let things cool off."

"This isn't the way it should have ended with H.T. He didn't deserve this!"

"What is done is done. The man is dead; that can't be changed. We have to make the best of it now!"

"I know. Still, I wish it could have been different."

"The man is dead, Amber! There is a lot to deal with if we are going to come out of this okay. We have to think about us now."

"Yes, you're right. But what about bills that need to be paid, papers that I need to sign, and money? Will I be able to get my money out of the bank?"

"I'll take care of all of that, Amber. Just go!"

"Okay."

"Provence?"

"No, the Grand Barrail Château Resort & Spa in Saint-Emilion." The memory of the Spa had come back to her in a flash. If she had to hide out, she might as well do it in a place that would cater to her every wish. She needed to be pampered.

"Good—that is perfect and while you're there, let's be smart about phone calls. I'll call you if we need to talk. Do not call me or the office unless I ask you to. For now, no e-mail either. Okay?"

"I have to trust you."

"You know you can."

"I truly hope so. I really, really, do."

CHAPTER 10

Sunday Afternoon

At breakfast Saturday morning, I had presented Dorin with a surprise bonus—a prepaid weekend for him and his wife at the Gaylord Opryland Hotel. Our hope was that they wouldn't be back before Monday afternoon. The husband and wife cleaned up the breakfast dishes and were out of the house and on their way to the hotel by 8:30 a.m. for the early check-in I had arranged.

The truth is that Sarah and I had decided that we really don't like having the live-in help arrangement. Getting the couple out of the house for the weekend was one of the best gifts I could give Sarah.

Sunday was family day—all twelve of us—children, spouses, and grandchildren. We decided on brunch at Old Natchez Country Club.

* * *

Now it was 2:30 p.m., and Sarah was taking a nap. So far I had kept my promise, but the weekend was almost over. I decided to make a phone call. It was time to find out what H.T.'s problem was all about.

The phone was answered on the fourth ring by Lansden's housekeeper: "Hola!"

A few years ago her Spanish would have caught me off guard. But around the Rollins family home, it was almost becoming a second language as we deal with gardeners and other workers.

"My name is Mark Rollins, and I would like to speak to Mrs. Lansden."

"Señora Lansden is away."

"You said Mrs. Lansden is away. Do you mean she has gone away on a trip—out of town?"

"Sí, señor. Would you like to speak to Mr. Tillman?"

That was unexpected. At least it seemed a little odd to me. I was curious. Why was Amber 'away,' and why was Paul Tillman, a law firm partner, in her house? "Yes, let me speak to him."

Tillman picked up the phone a couple of minutes later and said, "This is Paul Tillman. Can I help you?"

I reached into my memory bank and retrieved an image of Paul Tillman. He had been a basketball star in his college days. Now in his mid-forties, he had kept his athletic build. What had changed were the outward trappings: thick wavy salt-and-pepper hair, perfectly tailored pinstripe suits, custom-made shirts, and the finest Italian leather shoes. He is the leading man type, and while he is an attorney and not a movie star, he carries himself as if on camera at all times—straight, tall and perfectly groomed. There is something else about the man. He is rather patrician in how he relates to others. I remembered that he was well mannered enough, but there was an air of superiority or arrogance about him—maybe it was just the permanent smirk, almost a sneer, that he wore. Of course, the smirk could just be something he was born with. Time would tell.

It struck me that H.T. Lansden had hired men in his own image, tall and athletic. Although I must admit that while H.T. had lost some of that body tone over the years, Tillman had not. My guess is that Tillman spends time in the gym and even more in front of a mirror. I wouldn't be surprised if he was into youth hormones and steroids.

"Yes, Paul. This is Mark Rollins. How are you today?"

"Hello, Mark. I have been better, of course. This is a real tragedy for the law firm and the country. But the world keeps going around, and we are just on it for the ride."

"We are all sorry about H.T. He was a good man and a good friend. I was hoping to talk to Amber; is she available?"

"No. Apparently she decided to get away for a while. She left a message with my answering service saying she couldn't stay in their home another night—or handle another person wanting to rehash H.T.'s death."

"Do you know how long she will be away or where I can contact her?"

"The message indicated she was going abroad. Said she hadn't decided where she would stay or for how long. She made her flight reservations through the travel agency we use at the firm. I checked with them. She bought a ticket to Paris with an open return. I know that she and H.T. had a place where they liked to stay in Provence, but I don't remember the name of it. Is there anything I can help you with?"

"Not really; I wanted to discuss a personal matter with her."

"I'm handling Amber's affairs and taking care of the estate. In fact, that's why I'm here. Obviously, H.T. didn't have time to put his affairs in order. There are things I need. I would rather have had Amber get them for me, but since she isn't here, I've taken the liberty of searching through his home office and files. There is no one place to look any more. People have all kinds of things that are important for estate purposes—investments, lockboxes, insurance policies, and so on. You know, even credit cards can have an insurance component, especially in a case of accidental death."

"Accidental death?"

"What else would you call it? At least that is going to be our position with the insurance companies. He was shot, but clearly accidently. Never mind that, before I lose the point I was getting to, I have her power of attorney. If the reason you want to reach Amber has a business aspect, I'm sure I can take care of it for you."

"No, no—it's nothing like that. Actually, Paul, H.T. had called me the night before his death and said he had a problem, and he needed my help. I was hoping Amber could shed some light on that."

"What kind of problem?"

"I don't know. That is why I'm calling. He didn't want to talk about it on the phone so he made an appointment. He was killed before we could meet."

"And you don't know what he wanted to talk about?"

"No. Do you have any ideas, Paul?"

There was an unusually long pause before Tillman spoke. "I don't know, Mark. Whatever it was probably isn't important anymore."

The pause made me think that Paul was holding something back. I decided now was not the time to press the matter. He had been somewhat open with me so far, and I didn't want to change that. I said, "You are probably right, Paul. By the way, did you guys ever make the switch to a new software system? If I remember correctly, we were right on the verge of a deal just before I sold my company and retired."

His voice was much more relaxed as he replied, "No, we are still using the same old accounting system. The project died right after you got out of the business. Our administrator is change resistant, and you know how it is in a law firm. Other fires became more important. But I still can't get the reports I need when I need them. I get lots of paper but that is the problem. I don't have time to dig through all those pages and numbers, nor do the other partners. The law firm just seems to run itself okay. H.T. was the only one who could make sense out of the reports when he had time to spend on the financial side of our practice, which wasn't that often."

"Paul, I would be glad to spend a little time with your accounting people to see if we can get you the information you need—in a form that you can digest—even with your busy schedule."

"Have you started consulting, Mark?" he mused.

"No, in fact I'm under a non-compete agreement, but that does not stop me from helping good friends. I feel that I should do something to repay H.T. for the things he has done for me in the past. Law firm financial performance is something I know a lot about, and that includes providing busy partners with operational awareness in instantly digestible forms."

"I don't see how I can pass up that offer. Look, we have a partners' meeting on Monday. Let me discuss it with them, and I'll get back to you."

"Do you mind if I call to follow up?"

"You are right; I can get distracted by client work. If I haven't gotten back with you as promised, it doesn't mean I'm not interested in your proposal. You are welcome to take the initiative and call me."

"Paul, you said 'partners' meeting'. I thought there were just three of you. With H.T. gone, that would only leave you and Hall."

"No, we added a new partner just last month—Herbert W. Stewart III. We just haven't had time to change the letterhead and signage."

"I have heard of Herb Stewart, but I have never met the man. That is a real milestone for the firm, isn't it? I mean, adding a partner—isn't this a first? It has always just been the three founders."

"That's right. Herb is a talented and ambitious fellow. Cut from the same cloth as H.T.—and me for that matter—another tall jock. He and his wife were close friends of H.T. and Amber. They belonged to the same club—ran in the same circles. Amber and Herb grew up in the same neighborhood even dated some in high school days, I understand. The Stewarts live just a couple of houses over, and the two families did a lot together. H.T. pushed hard to convince Herb to take our offer to become a partner."

"I didn't know you had to twist people's arms to become a partner. Isn't that what all lawyers in private practice want?"

"Mark, that is true in most firms, but we have a very unorthodox compensation plan—one that H.T. dreamed up and has always insisted we stick with. Until now, the only thing the title of partner got you was a share of the risk."

"You said 'until now'?"

"Yes, Herb Stewart is one lucky man. H.T.'s death is going to produce a windfall for the remaining three of us. I'm almost embarrassed about it."

"How so?"

"Look, I'm really talking out of school. Probably shouldn't have said any of that. If the partners accept your offer, I can explain further; but for now, just consider those comments off the record and confidential."

"Of course. I'll let you get back to your detective work."

"My detective work? Oh, yeah.... You mean my search of H.T.'s office. Okay, Mark, I will get back to you about your offer—ASAP. And thanks again."

Paul Tillman and I ended our conversation. Amber was "getting out of Dodge." Running away from what?—well-wishers, reporters, or maybe curious police detectives? A windfall for the remaining partners... how does that compute? How much money are we talking about? Did anyone need it badly enough to kill for it? The questions were beginning to accumulate.

CHAPTER 11

Body by Brazil

Monday, I made it to the Club by 8:00 a.m. It was going to be the first time in quite a while that I put in a full day at the office. Not that I am really needed when it comes to running the place, but the members like to see me around. Ours is a unique and exclusive club. I'm part of the service. The role of "problem solver" is one that has evolved. Most of the time it is little more than a *Dear Abby* role. I listen and give straightforward, simple advice. Sometimes their problems, while very real to them, seem trivial or surreal. Some of the younger trophy wives don't have a lot of life experience to fall back on. Some come out of families that are far removed from the social and economic level into which the young women have married. With the absence of other female family members, they lack the support systems that most married women have.

I made the rounds, smiled, waved, and then retired to my office. I hadn't been there long before I looked up to see a mannequin of a young woman standing at the door to my office. She was resplendent in a stunning black tigress tank with matching pant. The black fitness outfit looked as if it had been painted on her Barbie doll figure. What made it striking were the stark white tiger appliqués—center chest on the tank top and twisting down the left thigh of the pant. I knew these pieces from watching a recent runway presentation of Body by Brazil's new couture collection. I love my job.

"Tess, you look gorgeous!" And she did. She had auburn hair and dark brown eyes. Her tan was smooth and silky, a light golden brown. I would put her in her early twenties. She is married to Tyler Brewster, a self-made man now so rich that even the blue-blooded Belle Meade crowd had accepted him as one of their own. Tyler was probably a nerd in high school. Later in life, being a nerd paid off big for him. He invented things. One of those things has to do with credit cards. As a result, he earns a royalty every time you use your card. "Come in and tell me what is going on in your life."

Her outfit said sex kitten, but as she came closer, I saw a pouting little girl. The leather guest chairs in my office are man-sized, making the little girl image even more pronounced. She retreated into one of the chairs, curling her legs under her. I half expected her to start sucking her thumb, but she didn't. With tearing eyes she whispered, "Tyler wants me to have a baby!"

"That's wonderful, Tess."

"No!" she rasped. "It is *horrible*. I would look *awful*. It would *ruin* my body. I could get *stretch marks*. I could lose my flat stomach. I just can't do that. I won't! *I won't do it, Mr. Rollins.*"

"Have you talked to Tyler about how you feel?"

"I tried... but he just said I was being ridiculous. That's easy for him to say. It isn't his body. I can't stand the thought of actually expelling a baby—they are so *big*! My body would never be the same again. What if Tyler wouldn't like me anymore?"

I could have said, 'Tess you can do this and still remain a beautiful woman,' but I knew that wouldn't fly with her. I decided to give her alternatives. "Tess, what about adoption? You could be like Madonna and Angelina Jolie. Offshore adoptions are in right now. People would envy both of you for doing such a courageous thing."

"I would do that. I would, but that wouldn't satisfy Tyler. He says he wants his legacy—his blood. And, he wants a son. I might have to get pregnant more than once to give him a son. I just *can't*. I would rather *die*! I really would."

"Tess, I know a California couple that hired a substitute to carry their baby to term. The process can be managed to insure that the baby is a male. Your eggs are fertilized *in vitro* with Tyler's semen and then the eggs are implanted into the surrogate mother. The surrogate goes through the nine months of pregnancy and gives birth. But, it's your DNA. It is *your* baby—yours and Tyler's. You might have to have it done outside the country, but it is very *avant-garde*. Tyler would get his son and keep his Tess just the way he likes you now."

"Can they really do that?"

"Yes, they can. There is the Surrogacy Center in the U.S. that will help arrange things for you and there are many options overseas. Tyler is a leading-edge kind of guy. He couldn't be the success he is without a willingness to take advantage of New Age things, and surrogacy is definitely leading edge stuff from both a medical and social aspect. Why don't I get you and Tyler some information about the process?"

"Mr. Rollins, he might really go for it! Would you talk to him for me?"

"I don't think that's a good idea, Tess. Guys don't like guys talking to them about their sperm."

"Yeah, you are right. It might be better if I get him in the mood first—make him appreciate me the way I am. Then I can show him the information. We could talk about it as a sure way to get what he wants, a son, without damaging my body. I think he would like that." She smiled and teasingly said, "He'd better, or I'll move to a separate bedroom."

I acknowledged her power, "That should do the trick!"

"We could hire a nanny. I could still travel with Tyler, play tennis, and do the country club. It wouldn't have to change our life that much, would it?" She smiled, uncurled from the chair, and said, "Thank you, Mr. Rollins." The woman that walked from the chair and out my door would have made the Body by Brazil people proud. She was no little girl—but was she right for motherhood?

It took me a few minutes to come back to the world in which Sarah and I are comfortable. Tess lives in a different one. As irresponsible as she might appear to people outside of that world, Tess believes her responsibility is to look beautiful. That is her contribution. To take that away from her is to take away her value as a person. I don't often question my decisions, but in this case, I could not help doing so. Is it right to bring a child into this world to be mothered by someone so narcissistic? I thought back to the period in England where the children of the upper classes were tended to by nannies—where the boys were packed up and sent off to boarding schools, returning home to reunite with their parents only at manhood. Great men and women traveled that road without apparent harm. Now times are different.

Nevertheless, Tyler is a smart man who wants a son badly. Knowing Tyler as I do, I can't imagine his son not receiving the love and attention a child deserves. Tyler might eventually have to make a choice between having a stunning Barbie doll on his arm and a caring mother for his child—or stepmother. I'm sure he will do the right thing for his son.

I looked down to make sure the lapel pin on my shirt pocket was still upside down. It was.

CHAPTER 12

Mariko's Assignment

Mariko burst into my office. Always the exhibitionist, Mariko's outfits tend to be on the theme side. Today she is wearing a bodysuit in deep purple with mid-calf boots. The black crushed leather boots have four-inch heels and lace up the front in Victorian style. Her hair shines. It is oiled, pulled back, and pressed tight against her head. She has a wide black belt riding just above her hips to support a set of full-flap handgun holsters—one on each hip. She turned around slowly so I could get the full effect of her outfit. While the skintight unitard is full-bodied in front, it has an open scooped back with crisscrossing straps. She was smiling broadly when she asked, "What do you think, Boss? Do I look like a Vice President?"

On anyone else, the costume would have looked ridiculous. But Mariko isn't anyone else. She is 5' 2" with zero body fat. Her personality is feisty and flirtatious. She could be sexy and deadly.

I answered, "Not on your life; nor would I ever want you to! Give me a minute.... Let me guess.... I've got it! I saw the movie with Billy Zane. You are The Phantom— *The Ghost Who Walks*. You are a new and quite improved model, I might add. But as is often the case, Mariko, your outfit doesn't leave room for you to hide anything."

"That's what the holsters are for." Placing her hand on the right side holster, she said, "My Beretta is in this one. The other one is for everything else—money, credit cards, carry permit, cell phone, lipstick, and all the other things a girl needs."

"Those holsters are authentic military issue—for the big .45 model 1911s—probably the most famous and reliable killing handguns ever made. Doesn't your 'little' Beretta Vertec get lost in there?"

"I had the inside customized at a local leather shop that builds holsters. They plugged the long toe and added leather to give the Beretta a perfect ride. They turned the other one into my purse."

"Okay Mariko, there has to be a reason for the outfit and the big smile. What gives?"

"I'm having a blast, Boss. Meg turned the new personal security classes over to me. I'm teaching our ladies how to break a few bones. We're doing some handgun training, too. That is really why I decked out as the great vigilante hero. You know, Boss, the ladies really dig this stuff. I think I'm creating some monsters. I hope no one's sugar daddy tries to get a little rough. If they do, they'll regret it!"

"Be careful, Mariko. Don't forget those sugar daddies are the ones paying our bills," I said jokingly.

"Wrong, Boss—at least for the next several months. Remember? You are giving everyone a free ride."

"Oh yeah, but that's just the membership fee. They still have to pay for miscellaneous charges and personal training sessions, and the truth is those aren't pocket change."

"Don't worry, Boss. Our members aren't worried about their spouses—it's the gangbangers, carjackers, and parking lot perverts that have them worried."

"Mariko, I hate to rain on your parade, but I may have an assignment for you that will take you away from your personal security classes for a couple of weeks."

"What is that, Boss?"

"After H.T.'s death, I set my Personal Digital Assistant software to track any news stories about H.T. Lansden's law firm. This morning one of the items that the PDA picked up was a want ad for an accounting clerk. I would like you to take that job. I'm not satisfied with the random shooting theory that the papers reported. If there is something sinister behind H.T.'s death, my guess is it's connected to the law firm. I would like to have someone on the inside gathering intelligence."

"What makes you think they would hire me?"

"I will call one of the partners, Paul Tillman. I'll tell him that you are a friend of the family and that I would like him to give you a try."

"Won't they want references?"

"You have them. We just have to put the right spin on things. You were in the Marines. When you completed your tour of duty, you enrolled in Vanderbilt's graduate school. Your dad died, making you a trust fund baby. After getting your MBA, you floated around for a while enjoying life. Did some personal training at the Women's Health Club. I knew about your MBA and hired you to work with me on a consulting project to help a prominent local law firm improve its financial performance. You proved to be a fast learner; showed exceptional insight into the key performance drivers that influence partner income. All of that is true, of course. Here is where we take a little departure from reality: I will tell Paul that you discovered you enjoyed working with numbers and working in a law firm environment. You have decided to pursue law firm financial management as a career, and you are willing to work your way up from the bottom."

"You think they will buy that?"

"Why wouldn't they? Paul isn't going to turn me down. He knows he can get rid of you if you don't work out. We are both businessmen. I would not expect him to do otherwise. He knows that."

"They won't think I'm there just to spy on them?"

"There is no reason for them to think that yet. They might later down the road, but we will cross that bridge when and if we have to."

"Okay, Boss. I'm game. What do you want me to do?"

"Other than boning up on your debits and credits and getting your accountant wardrobe in order, you don't need to do anything yet. I'm just giving you a heads-up."

"It won't be a problem. I took a bunch of accounting courses, and I learned a lot during our undercover consulting gig at the Parish Welch law firm. I still have the Hugo Boss suits unless you think they would be too MBA-ish."

"The power suits are probably too heavy. You don't want to scare the people you will be working with. Go shopping—but not in full *Phantom* uniform. While that outfit works here, in the mall it would cause a little more attention than even you would want."

"No problem, Boss. All I do is ditch the holsters and put on the matching Bluefish scuba-style jacket with a high neck, and I'm ready to go."

"Right! Like that jacket isn't just as formfitting as the bodysuit it is supposed to cover. You would just be another ordinary lady shopper wearing a skintight purple outfit and stiletto heels. You would blend right in. Wouldn't cause more than 40 or 50 guys to trip over their feet and catch hell from their wives for gawking at you!"

"Okay, Boss, I'll be a good girl. I'll go home and change to civilian duds before doing any shopping." She smiled, turned, and left my office.

CHAPTER 13

Settlement Gone Wrong

It was already Tuesday afternoon. As I half expected, Paul Tillman hadn't called. So I dialed him. The firm's receptionist put me through to his office.

"Paul, this is Mark Rollins."

"Sorry; our partners' meeting got shanghaied. We didn't get to your offer. The shit is hitting the fan regarding the Hudson Bluff Mortgage case."

"I remember the case. I read about it in the papers. It's another one of those sub-prime mortgage cases, isn't it?"

"Yes, and that is all we talked about in our meeting. It is *go or no-go* time. Hudson had wanted to settle all along and had talked big numbers. I can't figure out why H.T. was so intent on holding back. Maybe he was on a crusade. Now that he is gone, Hudson has dropped the size of its settlement offer. They seem to know what we have—and don't have—on them. In fact, I think they know our hand *too* well. That bothers me. They also know that without H.T., we don't have the same level of litigator talent. The client is pissed, of course. H.T. kept telling them, the Fenios, to hold out for a mega jury verdict. Now we are suggesting settlement, but for less than what Hudson had been offering at the beginning. We are between a rock and a hard place."

"It sounds like a tight spot. Anything I can do?"

"Not unless you can find a smoking gun for us. I'm thinking we should advise Mr. and Mrs. Fenio that, in view of H.T.'s death, they should consider moving their case to another law firm. Herb Stewart is pushing for a quick settlement. Hudson had been offering $5,000,000. We are still talking a lot of money, $2,000,000. Our take would be over $650,000. But from the client's viewpoint, they have lost $3,000,000. It's relative deprivation; nevertheless, to them it's real money. They will take it out on us. If we tell them to go to another law firm, and they opt to stay with us, at least that will pretty much take a malpractice suit off the table. If they go somewhere else, we are out the $650,000, but that may be the cheapest alternative."

"Would you continue with the court case if you had your smoking gun?"

"No, the client needs to settle. Let someone else be the crusader. I just want to get the mortgage company back to the five mill figure."

"Paul, if I understand the case, the critical question is: who misstated the Fenios' income? Did your clients lie? Or, did the Hudson representative fraudulently inflate the couple's income in order to qualify them for a loan he knew, without question, was far beyond their means?"

"That is the key to the case, but there is a bigger question. Did the Hudson representative carry out the fraudulent act on his own, or did he do it at the company's direction or with the company's knowledge? We have a lot of circumstantial evidence that this was standard operating procedure, SOP, for the company. There is a pattern of behavior, but in our particular case, we are still left with a 'he said, they said' case. H.T. believed he had the talent to win the case with what he had. Now, I don't know. Hudson showed some of their cards in our last meeting. They know the weakness in our arguments. They have been able to fabricate or legitimately come up with stuff that would bring into question some of the client's statements that H.T. was relying on."

"Look, can you give me a couple of days to do some research on my own? You may have heard that I have some rather unusual resources that I can tap. Maybe I can come up with your smoking gun, or if not, I might still be able to motivate Hudson to improve its offer."

"Mark, I don't know what you have in mind, but please remember that the means doesn't always justify the end—especially when you have to go before a judge in a court of law."

"Paul, I may not find anything; on the other hand, I might find just enough for you to persuade Hudson to put their five million back on the table."

"Give it a shot. If you find anything, I will owe you big time."

"I will get back with you sometime tomorrow with a progress report. And, Paul—before I let you go, I have a favor to ask. Have you filled that accounting position, yet?"

"No, we haven't. You are reading the want ads now?" he chuckled.

"I like to keep up with things. Anyway, I want to ask you to try a friend of mine in the job. Her name is Mariko Lee. She is a former Marine with an MBA from Vanderbilt."

"It sounds like she may be overqualified for this position, Mark."

"Maybe, but she hasn't had any on-the-job experience in a law firm other than a consulting project she worked on with me. I can tell you that she has a comprehensive understanding of the issues that determine per-partner income. She wants to pursue financial management in the professional services area, and she is willing to prove herself by working from the bottom up."

"We'll give her a try. I'll tell my administrator to stop his search and start her on the job. It will be up to her, of course, to keep the job. My administrator is Owen Santo. Actually, if you ask me, he's just a bookkeeper with a fancy title. Ms. Lee will be working for him. Have her give him a call to work out the details."

"Thanks, Paul. I'm pretty sure you will thank me later, but if I'm wrong, I wouldn't expect you to keep her on the payroll."

I thought it odd that Tillman would find it necessary to put Owen down by labeling him "just a bookkeeper." Administrators are usually the only person in the law firm who tries to keep it operating somewhat like a well-run business. They are hardly "just bookkeepers."

CHAPTER 14

The Dirt

As soon as the Tillman call ended, I buzzed Bryan.

Bryan answered in his own unique upbeat way, "Yo, Chief, what's up?"

"I have a project for you and your team."

"What's the priority?"

"For the next two days, it goes before everything else."

"Okay, give me the particulars."

"I'm looking for dirt on Hudson Bluff Mortgage, Inc. related to sub-prime mortgages—anything that implicates the company in fraudulent activities—particularly related to refinancing applications. More specifically, look for any communication between the mortgage company and their Nashville representative, one Edward W. Melbourne, which shows that the company was a willing participant in the falsification of loan applications in general and specifically related to the loan of Marcos and Angeline Fenio. I can use anything you find to my advantage even if it doesn't directly match the parameters I just gave you so cast a wide net."

"What are the rules of engagement?"

"We are talking cyber-collected intelligence only. You can go anywhere on the net and hack into any system, commercial, governmental, or personal."

Bryan chuckled as he asked, "You'll have the bail money ready, right?"

"Bryan, my boy, I forgot the most important part of my rules: don't get caught!"

"Roger, Chief."

"Bryan, keep me posted on your progress."

"Anything else?"

"Just get going. I need results ASAP."

I called Mariko next and told her the accounting job was hers and whom she needed to contact for her start date. Then I gave myself an assignment. I needed some thinking time. I didn't believe H.T. was killed by a wayward bullet. The question is: was his death premeditated murder or something else? Who killed him and why? It was time to make a list.

But first, I needed to give the little gray cells a rest, as Agatha Christie's Hercule Poirot would have said. It was time to go home, spend some time with my favorite lady, and relax with a perfect Skyy martini.

* * *

Sarah and I had a light dinner and retired to our den. The picture on the TV screen was interrupted by the message that I had an incoming call from the Women's Health Club. I was pretty sure the caller would be Bryan, and it was.

"Chief, is everything all right?"

"Why do you ask?"

"I was worried about you. I have some info for you, but it is after 10:00 p.m.; I didn't want to call if you guys had turned in for the night. Since you still have that chip implanted under your skin, I took a peek at your medical telemetry to see if you were still awake. According to the telemetry feeds, you are not only awake; you appear to be under considerable stress!"

"That's funny."

"How is that?"

"L.A. is about to be nuked, and you want to know if I'm okay?"

"What?" Bryan sounded completely baffled.

"We're watching Jack Bauer save the world. I purchased Season One through Six of the TV series *24* on DVD. Sarah and I don't watch TV on any regular schedule so we didn't watch the series when it was originally broadcast. Tonight, we stayed up to watch back-to-back segments of Season Two."

"Now I understand—," Bryan laughed, "one cliffhanger after another! Bauer never sleeps. Never goes to the head."

"If he pees, we could lose L.A. to the mushroom cloud! But let's get serious, Bryan. You must have found something important to have called this late."

"I have. Actually, I have several things—none hit a bull's eye, but are certainly interesting, and may give you something to work with. First, we have an e-mail from the company to all its representatives reminding them that they have no obligation to independently verify the applicant's stated income."

"That would imply they understood that the income figures were not always on the up-and-up."

"Chief, I don't get it. I don't understand why anyone would loan money without verifying the applicant's financial information. Whatever happened to the requirement that you had to provide the lender with copies of your W-2 and tax returns? That used to be standard procedure."

"All of those rules faded away under the weight of the ambitious goal to make homeownership more available to lower income individuals. Then we had the rise of the specialized mortgage company. They made the loans and then sold the mortgages. Once the people granting mortgages were no longer the same people who bore the consequences of default, there were no more constraints. The investigative checks disappeared. It was a short step from there to out-and-out falsification of the application."

"It's just amazing that we went down that road. Clearly a lot of people were asleep at the wheel."

"Agreed! Bryan, I take it that you haven't found anything that would prove the company actually condoned coaching applicants to inflate their income."

"Right. Nothing yet. But at a minimum, the company's policy seems to be '*don't ask, don't tell.*' Personally, I think it's code for '*do what you have to do to make the applicants qualify.*'"

"I agree with you, Bryan. It may be a gun, but it isn't smoking."

"We'll keep digging, Chief. We found something else that looks pretty important to me."

"What is it?"

"E-mail traffic between a Gmail account and Gordon Seemann, Chief Financial Officer of Hudson Bluff Mortgage. We used a keyword filter to search for chatter related to the particulars at issue. The Gmail traffic popped up near the top of our list due to that traffic's high frequency of hits against our search criteria. The Gmail account is a blind account, but we traced the traffic back to the point of origin. The e-mails originated from inside the law firm of Lansden, Tillman and Hall. This smells to high heaven. If the e-mail was aboveboard business communication, we wouldn't be talking about a blind e-mail account."

"It's more than just that, Bryan. Lawyers talk to lawyers. They don't talk directly to adverse parties. Can you tell who is using that Gmail account?"

"No. We traced it to a particular workstation but its network name is *Library System 2*. It appears to be a shared computer. Anyone in the firm could have had access to it."

"I assume whoever set up the account with Google did so using a bogus identity."

"Right, Chief."

"What about the contents of the e-mails? Do they tell us anything about the sender?"

"We know the Hudson sender, but there is nothing in the Gmail contents that gives us a clue as to the identity of the person inside the law firm. The first outgoing e-mail from the law firm had an attachment that appears to be a transcript of the initial interview between H.T. and the Fenios. There was no supplemental chitchat. The following day, Seemann responded. That e-mail was short and to the point:

> *Sample was good. Agree with arrangement.*
> *Requested package shipped. Ready for full delivery.*

There are five subsequent e-mails from the law firm to Hudson, each containing copies of a portion of the law firm's Fenio case file."

"So they bought, bribed, someone inside the law firm to feed them information. Now they have the complete playbook for the Fenios' case. And whoever it is, he is still keeping Hudson up-to-date."

"That's the way it looks, Chief."

"Alright, send me a copy of the e-mail from Seemann."

"Consider it done."

"Bryan, that e-mail said 'the package was shipped.' I assume Seemann is in the company's headquarters. Pull a list of shipments out of that office on the same day Seemann sent the e-mail. Stick with the usual shippers, UPS, Federal Express, etc. Hudson's source inside the law firm probably set up a mail drop under an assumed name. Nevertheless, if we filter the shipment list to isolate packages sent to locations within 100 miles of Nashville, it might lead us to the culprit. All we will need to do is check out each ship-to address until we ID Hudson's version of Deep Throat."

"Good idea, Chief."

"Also, Bryan, keep looking for evidence that implicates the company directly in loan application fraud. If they will bribe, they certainly wouldn't have a problem with a little perjury. If we find anything, we turn it over to the authorities."

"Roger that."

CHAPTER 15

Confrontation

It was 10:00 a.m. in New York. His secretary took my information and put me on hold.

A good three minutes passed before Hudson Bluff's CEO, Mr. Keith Nelson, came on the line.

"Mr. Rollins is it?"

"That's correct, Mr. Nelson. My Name is Mark Rollins."

"My secretary said you have some information about the Fenio case that is supposedly critical to my side— something for my eyes only, I believe."

"She got it right, Mr. Nelson."

"Alright, Mr. Rollins, I'm listening," he said slowly with an element of suspicion in his voice.

"I have documented proof that you have bribed a person inside of Lansden, Tillman and Hall to provide you with the Fenio case file."

"What the hell are you talking about—what kind of proof?"

"E-mails between Gordon Seemann and your inside source."

"What is your game, Mr. ...?"

"Justice for the Fenio family. All I want is for you to honor your initial settlement offer of $5,000,000. Do that, and they will settle. Everyone will be happy."

"Look, I don't know who you are or what you think you have, but I'll bet your ass I have more lawyers than you do. They can tie you up in knots. Whatever you think you have, they will dispute. Whatever you have, they will keep out of the courtroom—it will never see the light of day. So don't think for a minute we are going to roll over just because you ask nice. Our current offer is all the justice the Fenios deserve."

"I'm not asking nice. And I don't care about the courtroom. That's for someone else to pursue. What I have goes to the news media in time for tomorrow's nightly news unless you up the settlement to equal your original $5,000,000."

"Why should I give a shit?"

"The media goes into a feeding frenzy any time that they can nail a big bad corporate CEO. They will love this story—you on one side and the sad, disheartened Fenios about to lose their home on the other. Mr. Seemann's e-mail is going to be 'breaking news' on every network. That will just whet the media's appetite. They won't stop with the bribery story. First, it will be just the Fenios. Then the story will become all of the Fenio-like bad mortgage deals you put together.

Look, Nelson, I know you're not worried about the Fenio case. It's peanuts. I know it, and you know it. You're worried about a class action suit. Believe me, when the newspeople are through with your carcass, the lawyers will start chewing on the bones. You'll be fighting off so many different lawsuits that a class action will start to look good to you."

"Alright, I get it. All you want is the original settlement?"

"There is one other thing that is non-negotiable. You have to give up your source inside the law firm. That's the only way I can keep from taking this to Lansden, Tillman and Hall or the media."

"How do I know it will stop here? What will keep you from asking for money next time or going public with your allegations after I have met your conditions?"

"You have my word."

"What the hell is that worth?"

"Give me the name of someone you trust absolutely."

"What kind of name?"

"Anyone's—another businessman, someone from the military, intelligence service, government, or even your church. It doesn't matter as long as you trust them."

"Okay ... Colonel Baker, Jeremy Baker."

"Yes. He is a distinguished U.S. Army officer currently on the faculty at West Point. I know him well. Call him and ask if my word is worth anything."

"I will. If he says I can rely on your word, you will have your $5,000,000 settlement, and we will encourage our inside guy to resign."

"You will have to do more than encourage; I want his name."

"Okay, Rollins, I'll give you his name once the settlement is a done deal."

"Agreed."

"I'm curious, Rollins, what if you had not known the Colonel?"

"There aren't that many people in this world that can be trusted completely. I know most of them. But if the Colonel had not been one, I would have put him in touch with someone who is among that elite group."

"I suppose you're telling me you are one of them?"

"I am."

Our phone call ended. The Fenios would get their settlement, and the firm would get rid of a dishonest lawyer in their ranks. But I wasn't happy. Hudson Bluff Mortgage didn't deserve to get off so easily. They won't if I can help it. I gave Nelson my word about the bribery, but that will not stop me from turning over evidence that they have engaged in other illegal activities. It's up to Bryan to find that evidence.

CHAPTER 16

Euros

"Gordon!" Nelson shrieked. "You have been busted! Now we have to give up our Fenio source, and I have to push my damn settlement offer back up to the original $5,000,000!"

"What do you mean 'busted'?"

"Some guy named Rollins called. He has copies of your fucking e-mails to that Maxwell guy!"

"How does he know it was Maxwell?"

"What do you mean?"

"I mean the e-mails involving the case file never identified who the supplier was. He used one of those Gmail addresses that anybody can set up in a minute or less. I know the e-mails didn't identify Maxwell because I was already becoming concerned that he might not be working alone."

"What are you talking about? Spit it out, man!"

"I was going to call him about the General Counsel position, but he called me first with the offer to sell us the Fenio file. He sounded different over the phone. Said he had a cold so I let it go. But it made me start thinking that maybe Maxwell wasn't working alone. After that phone call, we communicated by e-mail, but it was that Gmail address so anybody could have been at the other end of the computer."

"But it *was* Maxwell, right?"

"It had to be Maxwell or someone in on it with him. Who the hell else could it have been? But I can tell you this: I don't think Maxwell was ever interested in a job with us. I think he intended to hit us up for cash all along."

"You had to pay Maxwell or somebody—*who* did you give our money to?"

"We sent cash to one of those private mailboxes."

"You sent fifty fucking thousand in cash?"

"Actually, they were euros."

"What the hell did he want euros for?"

"I don't know. He called on the phone; said he could get us the file. Then followed up by e-mail; sent us a sample. For roughly $65,000 in U.S. dollars, it was cheap—a no-brainer—so we followed his instructions. Whoever he was, he delivered the file as promised."

"I don't get the euro thing."

"Mr. Nelson, maybe it is a way around the U.S. banking laws. He deposits the euros offshore to get around the reporting requirements that U.S. banks have."

"How did you come up with fifty thousand euros?"

"We had about twenty thousand in our travel fund in the vault. The rest I got from five different banks to stay under their reporting requirements. Told them we needed euros for travel purposes."

"Where did you ship the money?"

"A UPS® Store in Spring Hill, Tennessee."

"Where the hell is that?"

"I think it's about 50 miles south of Nashville."

CHAPTER 17

Parker McGovern

"Thank you for seeing me, Mr. Tillman."

"We want to be helpful, Detective McGovern. H.T.'s death was a great loss to us. We don't want something like this to happen to anyone else. Whoever that drunk was, we need him off the streets. There are too many damn guns in this country, and too many of them are in the hands of reckless and irresponsible people like that intoxicated idiot."

"Yes, sir."

"What would you like from us, Detective?"

"We want to interview your people. It's routine in any homicide. We need to touch every base."

"I don't understand." Tillman sounded irritated. "We know what happened to H.T. He was killed by a stray bullet from a stoned nitwit who was emptying his gun in the air like some Middle Eastern raghead—total disregard for the safety of everybody around him."

"Yes, sir, but we have our procedures. We just can't accept things as they appear on the surface. It's our job to determine what we are dealing with. We haven't found the shooter yet. When we do, who knows, this could turn out to be something different from what it first appears. Maybe we're dealing with a disgruntled client of yours who only pretended to be drunk. There is a big difference between criminal negligence, which this appears to be on the surface, and first-degree murder. It's our job to figure out which one we are dealing with."

"Of course, you do realize, Detective, that I cannot force any of our people to talk to you."

"I understand; however, I would be surprised if anyone objected. I trust you will convey to your people that this is a routine investigation and that the law firm encourages everyone to cooperate with the authorities."

"I'm a lawyer, Detective McGovern." The irritation was still there. "You can't expect me to tell my people to march into your interview room like a bunch of sheep. I will advise them all right, but that advice will be that they have the right to decline your request for a voluntary interview. They can agree to the interview but decline to answer any particular question. With regard to any interrogation, voluntary or involuntary, they always have the right to have a lawyer present, or if they initially waive that right, they can stop the interview at any point until such time that they do have their lawyer present."

"It's the 'Cops and Lawyers' is it? I'm a cop. My job is to put the bad guys away. You are a lawyer. Your job is to make my job more difficult. Right, Mr. Tillman?" McGovern's tone conveyed his disdain.

"I don't agree. I'm an officer of the court. My obligation is to protect the rights of citizens and make sure that justice prevails."

"Yeah, Tillman, that is the way it reads—we are all supposed to be pursuing justice. But there are bad cops, bad lawyers, and liberal judges. It doesn't always work the way it is supposed to."

"Ours is an adversarial system," Tillman said with an air of superiority. "I happen to think it is better as a result."

"Whatever you say, sir. You do what you think you need to do to protect your people's rights and let me get on with my job." McGovern was tired of this pompous ass.

"Alright, Detective, what do you want from me?"

"A room for my interviews and a list of your people."

Paul Tillman picked up his phone and buzzed his secretary. "Mrs. Harcourt, I have Detective Parker McGovern with me. Find an available conference room for him to use for the rest of the day. Also, get a current roster of our people—partners, associates, and everyone else. I also want you to prepare a memo from me to everyone in the firm advising them that, as a part of the authorities' routine investigation of H.T.'s death, Detective McGovern would like to interview all of us. Get Herb Stewart to assist you. I want the memo to spell out the rights of the interviewee. Stewart will know what to put in the memo."

Tillman listened for a few minutes and then said, "Good idea; put phone extensions on the list. And, yes, I want to review the memo before we distribute it. That's all for now."

He ended the call and turned back to face the detective. "Mrs. Harcourt has reserved Conference Room Number Four for you. Give her about ten minutes and your list should be waiting for you in the conference room."

"Do you mind if I ask you a few questions first?" McGovern thought he'd better take advantage of this opportunity while he still had an audience with Tillman.

"Go ahead, but please keep it brief. I have clients that require my attention."

"Do you own a gun?"

"Yes."

"It doesn't appear to be registered; I checked."

"It's a hand-me-down from my father, but the pistol originally belonged to my grandfather who acquired it long before gun stores were required to report purchases."

"What's the make and caliber?"

"It is a Smith and Wesson .38, a revolver. In its day, it was the standard service weapon for the policeman on the beat."

"That's right. Those were the days before we became out-gunned by the bad guys in the world. Does that mean your grandfather was one of us, Mr. Tillman?"

"Yes, for the city of Nashville before it became a Metropolitan Government in 1963. He retired in '58."

"Where do you keep the handgun?"

"Detective, I don't care much for this fishing trip you are on. I don't see how my gun is relevant, but I'll satisfy your curiosity. It's here in my desk where I always keep it."

"Do you have a carry permit?"

"No, but I'm an owner of this law firm. Under Tennessee law, the owner of the enterprise may lawfully have a loaded handgun on the premises. I think you can agree our office is not located in the safest neighborhood. And, of course, I'm a lawyer—not everyone or every client is always happy with my work. I keep it here for my personal protection."

"Yes, Mr. Tillman, you do have the legal right as long you don't carry the loaded weapon off of the premises. May I see it?"

Tillman opened his desk drawer and withdrew the handgun, then handed it butt first to the detective.

McGovern inspected the gun confirming that it was loaded. He opened the cylinder and removed the cartridges. He reclosed the cylinder and then looked down the barrel. The detective placed his finger against the muzzle end of the barrel, pressed, and twisted his finger. He withdrew his finger and held it up for Tillman to see the black circle on his fingertip. "Mr. Tillman, that is gunpowder residue. When is the last time this gun was fired and where?"

"Detective, I have *never* fired that gun! And, I have never cleaned it. Look at the ammo. The bullets in that gun are probably at least 50 years old!"

"Would you agree to sign the weapon out to me for testing so I can confirm that it has not been fired recently?"

Tillman hesitated. McGovern raised his eyebrows. Seeing he had no real choice, the law firm partner relented. "If you insist, but I still don't understand *why*."

"Just humor me, sir. When we have a handgun crime, we like to test all of the weapons we come across in our investigation. That's why they call us detectives—we detect."

"That is absurd!" Tillman said impatiently. He wanted this interview over and his dismissive voice conveyed that message clearly. As far as Tillman was concerned, McGovern was just another under-educated bureaucrat. He was no threat to Tillman. "Take the damn gun. Hell, it might not even work anymore. Run whatever tests you want to. You're just wasting your time and mine."

McGovern wouldn't be put off so he continued... "Just a couple more questions. Where were you at the time of the shooting?"

"I was up against a Monday court deadline so Sunday turned into a work day. I was in my office from about 2:00 p.m. until 9:45 p.m. I left the firm just minutes before it all happened. I picked up my car from the parking garage and drove home."

"You live in Belle Meade, right?"

"Yes."

"What time did you arrive home?"

"I'm not sure, but I drove straight home ... except for stopping for gas at a BP station close to St. Thomas Hospital."

"Did you use a credit card?"

"No, Detective, I paid with cash."

"Isn't that a little unusual in this day and time?"

"I use full service whenever I can. I don't like credit cards. I don't like the smell of gasoline. And, I don't like these personal questions!"

"Okay. Let's talk about building security. I noticed you have a key card entry system."

"Yes, it's magnetic, I suppose. We each have a card. You place it near the panel beside the doors to enter the building. The receptionist can admit people with a switch during business hours. After that, the only way you can enter the building is by using your key card."

"What about exiting the building?"

"You don't need to use your card. The last person leaving the building at night has to set the alarm, but that doesn't require the card either. You just enter a code number. It's the same code for everyone."

"That kind of system keeps a record of who entered the building, doesn't it?"

"Yes, Detective, each card has a unique ID number and we keep track of who each card belongs to."

"I would like a printout of who entered the building and at what time on the night H.T. was shot."

"I'll ask Mrs. Harcourt to get that from our technical staff. She will bring it to you when it's ready."

"Thank you, Mr. Tillman. I'm ready for that conference room now."

"Mrs. Harcourt will show you where it is. Her cubicle is directly across from my office door."

CHAPTER 18

Mariko's First Day

Sarah and I finally convinced Gabriela that variety is the spice of life. That is how Sarah explained today's breakfast menu. Frankly, I think our live-in help is getting even with her for insisting that she abandon her day-of-the-week approach to menu planning. This morning's breakfast consisted of steamed rice and miso soup accompanied by little pieces of boiled fish and nori. I recognized the nori, dried seaweed, which one eats by first dipping it in soy sauce and rolling a little rice in it. Yum. Yum. I went for the sliced Fuji apple reluctantly provided by Gabriela to placate my dear wife, who thankfully continued to insist that breakfast always include a fruit dish.

My breakfast was interrupted by a phone call—which was okay by me. I left the nori to Sarah and retreated to my sunroom office to take the call.

"Mark, it's Paul Tillman. Hudson's attorney called last night. They have reinstated their original $5,000,000 settlement offer. Mr. and Mrs. Fenio have agreed, and we will be signing the papers in a few days. Do I have you to thank for this development?"

"Let's just say I had a chat with the CEO."

"I also wanted to talk to you about something else. Do you know a Detective Parker McGovern?"

"I know of him, but I have had no personal contact with him. Why do you ask?"

"He was in our office yesterday interviewing our people. He's coming back again today. I get the feeling that he thinks there is something more to H.T.'s death than just an errant round from the gun of a drunk. One of the people he interviewed yesterday was Bill Maxwell, a talented senior associate. When I came in the office early this morning, his resignation letter was on my desk—gave us the usual two-week's notice. I hope that isn't related to McGovern's investigation. I was wondering if you had heard anything."

"Paul, I suspect McGovern is just following the department's playbook."

"I was wondering if you would talk with him—find out what is going on."

"Paul, he is just doing his job. Besides, if I did talk to him, I wouldn't be able to divulge any particulars. I have a unique relationship with our various law enforcement groups. It's a relationship based on strict confidentiality."

"I understand. There doesn't seem to be any doubt about what happened so I don't understand why all the questions. He could complicate our insurance claim."

Paul and I ended our phone conversation. I decided to check with Mariko. It was still early so I called the number for her condo.

"Good morning, Boss. Five minutes earlier and you would have gotten my answering service. I was in the shower. Why call so early?"

"Sorry, Mariko. I wanted to ask you how your first day at the law firm went. I just got off the phone with Tillman. He seems nervous about the police interviews."

"He's not the only one. The guy I report to, Owen Santo, didn't seem overly happy to have me forced on him to start with, and when he learned that there was a detective interviewing people, he got *very* antsy. Spent a lot of time talking to people who had already been interviewed, trying to find out what questions the detective was asking."

"Anyone else strike you as unusually concerned?"

"The new partner, Herbert Stewart, was in and out of Santo's office all day long. I couldn't tell what they were talking about, but Santo was animated and Stewart didn't look like a happy camper. I got the feeling that Santo was keeping him posted on the interviews. Tillman stopped by Santo's office a couple of times as well, but it appeared to be about routine business stuff."

"Did you learn any more about the company's compensation plan?"

"No, I didn't. The problem yesterday was that Santo was so distracted that I didn't get a chance to spend much time with him. I did go to lunch with another member of the accounting staff, Carolyn Osburn. She is in her fifties, has been at the firm for seventeen years so she is a knowledgeable source, and seems eager to take me under her wing. She filled me in on the history and personalities at lunch. I spent the afternoon playing second chair to her while she reviewed the firm's billing and disbursement procedures. I'm planning to go to lunch with her again today."

"How did the procedures seem to you?"

"Boss, you will love this! I know the accounts payable system they are using. You can buy it off the shelf in any of the big chain office supply stores. It's loose as a goose. The system will actually let you change check information *after the fact*. For example, I could write a check to myself. The next day or next week, I could edit the computer record to replace my name with the name of a legitimate supplier and rerun the check register. As far as the company's records are concerned, everything would look perfectly proper."

"Mariko, if the law firm is on its toes, they would discover the skullduggery when the cancelled checks arrive with the law firm's bank statements."

"That assumes that the person reconciling the bank statement to the law firm's books is not the same person misappropriating funds. Boss, you know how law firm's are! They don't have a big accounting department, and they aren't strong on internal controls. I would *love* to get my hands on their bank statements and cancelled checks."

"I assume you are talking hypothetically. You don't actually have any evidence that someone is embezzling funds, right?"

"All I know is that the opportunity is there. It's just begging for someone to take it."

"Mariko, I would guess that the someone you have in mind is your boss."

"Yes, he approves invoices for payment; he signs checks, except those over $25,000; *and* he reconciles the bank statements. How is that for top notch internal control?"

"I see what you mean. If Santo is dipping into the till and Lansden discovered it, we could have a motive for murder. *That* is worth checking out. I will have Bryan find out if your boss is living beyond his means. See if you can find out where the old bank statements are kept. Maybe you can arrange to work late some night."

"Will do."

"Mariko, I have another call waiting. I'll check with you again later today."

"Okay, Boss."

I pressed the call-waiting button and Tony was on the line. "Good morning, Mr. R. What time will you be wanting my services this morning?"

"It is already nine o'clock, Tony. Give me thirty minutes. And we might need to stop at McDonald's on the way for a McMuffin."

"I understand. I drove Gabriela to an international food store yesterday. How about I fix you an egg sandwich in my little kitchen? You can enjoy it and a cup of coffee on our way to the Club."

"Tony, my man, that is a great plan. Let's do it!"

CHAPTER 19

Sam Littleton

Sarah and I had a little chitchat as I walked out the front door to the waiting Lexus. We agreed on a plan to get our house back.

* * *

I finished the last of the egg sandwich just as Tony and I arrived at the Club. There was a traffic jam as departing and arriving cars fought over the shared entrance to the Club's back parking lot. Boot campers and early bird Pilates trust fund daughters were trying to leave just as the more leisurely late-sleepers were beginning to arrive from Belle Meade. I made a note to have a separate exit constructed.

Eventually, Tony let me out at the front door of the building because I wanted to talk to Shannon at the reception desk. She was wearing a big smile as usual.

"Good morning, Shannon. How is your 'Save the Children' project coming?"

"Oh, I'm working on something else now."

"What is that?"

"Right now, it's a secret, but I know you will want to help when I can tell you about it."

"I'm sure I will, Shannon. I'll have my checkbook ready. Right now, I have a project of my own that I need your help with. I want you to find an apartment for me. Actually, it's for a couple. The husband is a graduate student at Vanderbilt so it needs to be something close to the university. I need it for six months, and I will be the person paying the lease. Can you do that for me?"

"Sure thing. How much do you want to pay?"

"See what you can find for under $2500 a month."

"Gee, Mr. Rollins, you don't want an apartment, you want a *mansion!*"

"Believe me, at any price, this will be worth it to me. I do want something nice. A one bedroom, one bath would be fine. If you find something for less than $2500, I will be even happier."

"Who is this lucky couple?"

"A foreign exchange student and his wife—I invited them to stay with us during a senior moment when I wasn't thinking straight. Now I want my house back."

"How soon do they want to move in?"

"The sooner the better."

* * *

When I got to my office, I called Sam Littleton. As usual, he answered my phone call himself.

"Sam, it's Mark Rollins."

"I know. Your name came up on my display. Of course, that's why you are talking to me and not my voice mail."

"Thanks. I need a favor."

"What can the FBI do for you today?"

"Do you know Parker McGovern?"

"Homicide Detective in the MNPD."

"The what?"

"Oh yeah, I forgot you have a thing about acronyms— that's the Metropolitan Nashville Police Department to you."

"Right. Do you know him?"

"Sure do, Mark. We have worked with him on a couple of things."

"He is investigating the death of Harold T. Lansden who was supposedly shot by some drunk down in Printers Alley the other night."

"I remember reading about that incident. He is a good man, Mark."

"I have a particular interest in the case and would like to know where his investigation stands. Would you give him a call and let him know who I am? Encourage him to share his info with me."

"Be happy to. But I need to know if this is strictly for you and your team. You're not acting on anyone else's behalf, are you?"

"It is for our eyes and ears only. H.T. was a good friend of mine. I'm not comfortable with the random shooting story. If there is something sinister here, I want to make sure that bad guys don't get away with his murder."

"What is in it for McGovern? Why should he tell you what his investigation has uncovered so far?"

"Sam, you know me and my team. We've been doing some investigating on our own. We can tell him what we have been able to dig up."

"Do you think you have something material to his case?"

"What I have are pieces. McGovern has pieces. If we put them together, we might have enough pieces to solve this puzzle."

"Mark, that is the way it has been when you and I have worked together. That's what I'll tell McGovern. When you and I have shared our intel, we have solved cases. I think that will do the trick for him."

"Good. Let me know when I can give him a call to set up a meeting. Better yet, why don't you join us in the meeting? That would make it more comfortable for McGovern. I'm sure he has people looking over his shoulder. With you there, he can say that he briefed the FBI. Putting that in his report will read a lot better than 'I shared intelligence with an ordinary civilian.'"

"Right you are, Mark. Let's let him cover his butt. That's the way I will play it with him. I will set up the meeting and let you know when and where."

"Thanks, Sam."

CHAPTER 20

Bryan's Intel

I called Bryan after getting off the phone with Sam. I needed red meat to give McGovern.

"I'm glad you called, Chief. I just wrapped up a meeting with my team. We have come up with a number things that will interest you."

"Let's have them."

"Let's start with the package from Hudson. Finding the ship-to location was a slam dunk. Frankly, it was almost too easy."

"How so?"

"The package was shipped to Harold T. Lansden by way of a private mailbox at a Spring Hill, Tennessee, UPS Store. I sent one of my guys to the store to ask a few questions. The package was picked up by a Bill Maxwell using a power of attorney signed by our dead attorney.

Maxwell also cancelled the lease on the mailbox while he was there."

"Very interesting."

"That's not all. We decided to check around Spring Hill for anything else in Lansden's name or under the name of any of the other people in our keyword search criteria. Guess what? Lansden has a lockbox at one of the local banks. The fact that he had a U.P.S. mailbox and a lockbox in Spring Hill, which was nowhere near his home or office, means he was keeping secrets."

"So you don't think some third party was surreptitiously using Lansden's name to rent the boxes?"

"No, we showed the clerk a copy of the newspaper obituary with Lansden's picture. The clerk recognized him as the man who rented the box about a month ago."

"Then someone who knew about the mailbox used it to take delivery of the package."

"Right, Chief, I assume that was this Maxwell person."

"That is how it would appear. He gave his two-weeks notice this morning. When Tillman told me about the resignation, I took that to ID him as the mole who sold the Fenio file to the mortgage people. But how would Maxwell have known about the mailbox? That's what I don't understand. He was only a senior associate at the law firm. He could just be a patsy set up to take the fall."

"But, Chief, *he* is the guy who picked up the package."

"Yeah, maybe he is the mole, or maybe he is only a gofer. He could have picked up the package for someone else."

"Well, that would have to be someone up the corporate ladder, so to speak, wouldn't it?"

"Yes, or he was doing it for a friend, lover, or co-conspirator. Bryan, I'm going to have to do some digging on my end to see where the dots lead me. What else do you have for me?"

"Plenty. Their roster of people plays like a TV soap opera. The new partner, Herbert Stewart, is a lady's man with an appetite for gambling. He is a big player—a regular in Atlantic City and occasionally slums in Tunica. He is married but that doesn't seem to stop him from being seen frequently with a model-type on his arm. Reports are he goes for the enhanced types. I found a lot of party pictures on the Web featuring our man. He looks the lawyer part, but Stewart just doesn't seem like the kind of person Lansden would want as a partner in his firm—if for no other reason than the bad publicity he could gin up. My guess is somewhere, sometime, Stewart is going to make the kind of news a law firm wouldn't want. Let's start with the fact that he is up to his neck in debt and some of his creditors are the kind of people that don't wait patiently in line to be paid."

"So he is high on the list of those needing that windfall Tillman was talking about."

"Right-O! And, it is *some* windfall. My guess is that the prospect of that money is the only reason his gambling friends haven't already busted his kneecaps. They are lining up to get theirs as soon as the insurance company pays off. The firm had a $10,000,000 key man policy that doubles in the event of accidental death. $5,000,000 goes to the widow, regardless. The balance is shared equally among the partners. Herby-boy walks into a cool third of $15,000,000 if Lansden's death is ruled an accident. Even if it isn't, he still gets a little over a million and a half."

"Speaking of the widow, how important is the $5,000,000 to her?"

"Chief, Harold Lansden was making over a million dollars a year as a partner in the law firm. He and his wife lived pretty darn well. He had built a sizable estate prior to the stock market tumble. Unfortunately a lot of that was in GM stocks and bonds."

"Bryan, you know the old saying, 'As GM goes, so goes the country'? GM's down the tubes and the current crop of idiots in D.C. are dragging us down with it."

Bryan chuckled, "At least you are being bipartisan. You don't care if they're a Democrat or Republican; you want to throw all the bums out. But, getting back to the widow, I don't see how the insurance money would be a motive for Mrs. Lansden to do in her husband because he was worth more to her alive than dead. The five million is damn important now, but that's because she won't have the million-plus her hubby was pulling out of the law firm every year. Even with the insurance money and what is left of their investments, she is going to have to go on a budget."

"Bryan, there are a lot of people in this world that would find the idea of a budget, in her case, humorous. You can get by just fine with a few million in the bank."

"I wasn't being literal, Chief. My point is that there would have to be another reason if she is involved in her husband's death. It wouldn't make sense to kill him for the insurance money."

"It would certainly seem that way. The fact that she appears to have run away to Europe does make you wonder, however. What if H.T. was about to divorce her, for example? That might explain the mailbox and the lockbox. Have you had any luck finding her?"

"Zero, Chief. She apparently isn't using her credit cards, at least the ones we know about. We are doing a search on hotel records concentrating primarily on the ones in France. She is either not in France, or she is staying somewhere that does not use an online reservation system. There are a lot of small bed-and-breakfast places over there and then you have the villas you can rent—all without leaving a cyber trail."

"Keep searching. Try French car rentals or car services. I also want you to look for any indication that Mr. and Mrs. Lansden were not living in complete marital bliss. One or the other could have wandered from their marital vows."

"Will do, Chief. I have more info for you, but I need to take a break. Unlike Jack Bauer, there are times when the facilities call my name and this is one of those times."

"Okay. Give me a buzz when you are ready to pick up where we are leaving off. I'm eager to hear what you have on Santo."

CHAPTER 21

Swine Flu

While Bryan was taking a break, I decided to touch base with Meg. She was in her office with a towel around her neck. Her hair was damp. "Hello my favorite daughter; you look like you're cooling down."

"Oh. Hi, Dad. Yes, I subbed for one of the aerobics instructors. The rule is if you are sick, don't come to work. Same rule applies to our members. If you are sick, stay home!"

"Ha, I thought you had just been working out. I had almost forgotten for a moment just how scared everyone is about this 'swine flu' thing. I hope it's just overblown— but Obama is pulling out all the stops. He had a press conference this morning alerting people that we might have to close the schools. If the danger is real, I have to give him good marks for his quick action. I would prefer it to be just another case of his mantra 'Never let a crisis go to waste'."

"Dad, you remember what happened the last time we had a flu outbreak—and that was just the *regular seasonal stuff* that we always deal with. We almost closed the Club! So don't underestimate the problem. Fitness facilities are fertile ground for viruses. I want to put in my vote now— at the first real sign of swine flu, we close for a couple of weeks to protect our members and staff."

"Okay, you are right, but let our members participate in that decision. You know how it is, if we announce a decision to close the Club out of the blue, we will get blamed for every ounce of weight gain. If it's their idea to close down for their own protection, we are off the hook."

"Good idea, Dad. We will introduce the idea of contingency plans on the blog. I'll also print up a flyer to hand out at the reception desk. That will condition them to the fact that something will have to be done. Then I'll run an online survey, publish the results, and communicate our plans for dealing with an outbreak."

"Sounds perfect, Meg. Anything else I need to know about?"

"Just that things seem to have calmed down since we put out the notice waiving the membership fee. The concerns have dried up. Of course, we have also had a big point increase in the Dow. That probably helps, too."

"Yes, but that still means the average cumulative losses for equity investors is around 40%. The market is just back to where it was when Obama took office."

"At least the direction has been up lately and that makes people feel better."

"Yes. Up is better than down. I'm going back to my office to make some phone calls, but if you need anything, Meg, just yell."

"Okay, Dad. And, tell Mom I might need her help with the children if they close the schools."

"Will do."

CHAPTER 22

Tillman's Invitation

When I got back to my office, there were two messages on my phone. The first was Bryan telling me he was ready for me. The second was from Paul Tillman. I selected the option on the phone to return Tillman's call. It was his direct line. He answered, and obviously his phone, like most business systems these days, displayed the name of the caller.

"Mark, thanks for returning my call. We are trying to get back to normal. If your offer to give us a hand still stands, my partners want to accept. Could you join us Monday for a 10:00 a.m. partner meeting? Hall and Stewart were both pretty vocal about the need for better information, especially with H.T. out of the picture."

"I'll be there. I will put together some examples of what I think will help you. But I warn you, you may have to upgrade your computer software to get what you really need."

"We will see. Frankly, I am not too anxious to deal with a big computer conversion. In fact, I'm thinking about calling it quits—letting Hall and Stewart take it from here."

"Paul, I tried retirement once. Frankly, it's not what it is cracked up to be."

"With the insurance from H.T.'s death, I can afford to take it easy for awhile."

"Why not just take a long vacation?"

"That's easier said than done, Mark. If you still have client responsibility, you can never get away. We're chained to our cell phones, BlackBerrys, and laptops. Hell, I've taken calls from clients while on the toilet. No, the only way is to give it up all together. Let the new blood take over."

"So you would walk away from your share of the firm's income?"

"Not completely. Everyone in our firm, associates as well as partners, earn origination fees for life as long as they remain a part of the firm. If you retire, there is a seven-year phase-out plan. Technically you remain a member of the firm during that time to get around some of the ethics rules dealing with fee sharing."

"What about H.T.? Does Amber get the seven-year buyout?"

"No, everything stops when you die. Except for her $5,000,000 share of the insurance money, she won't receive anything else from the firm."

"Paul, H.T. was drawing down over a million a year. If that stops, and there is no buyout, doesn't that mean the remaining partners just got a big raise?"

"Yes, but it won't be as big as you might think. We will probably lose many of the clients H.T. was taking care of personally. We will keep some of them, but the work will be done by attorneys with a smaller hourly rate than what H.T. was able to command. And now that we have Herb as a partner, whatever margin increase we have will have to be split three ways. That is just it, Mark. It is too much change to deal with."

"My advice, Paul, is that you think long and hard before you decide to spend the rest of your life on the beach."

"I just wanted to let you know that I'm thinking about it. I haven't said anything to Hall or Stewart. For now, I would like to keep it that way."

"Sure. Paul, have you heard anything from Amber?"

"I received a couple of e-mails from her basically telling me she's okay but isn't ready to come back to Nashville yet. Said she is still trying to deal with the loss of H.T."

"Do you know where she is staying?"

"No I don't; she didn't say."

"Can you send her an e-mail telling her I still want to talk to her? Have her call me on my cell."

"I can't do that, Mark."

"Why not?"

"She doesn't have her computer with her, and her cell isn't equipped for international use."

"How did she e-mail you then?"

"The e-mails were from an Internet coffee shop and she used an e-mail form without a return e-mail address."

"Can you forward them to me? Maybe we can trace them back to their source."

"Sorry, Mark, I deleted them. If she e-mails me again, I'll forward them to you at that time."

"I don't understand, Paul. Why is she *incognito*? Her behavior is not normal for a grieving widow. Frankly, she just didn't seem that upset at the memorial service."

There was a strange pause on the other end of the line before Paul Tillman said, "All I can tell you, Mark, is that she said she had to get away for awhile. We've been so busy with everything else; I just haven't given her behavior much thought. Maybe she is depressed. I hadn't thought about it before. That might account for the mood swings—seeming to be happy at the memorial and then running off to be alone. I hope she isn't in danger... you know... of hurting herself. I had better start trying to find her. I'll let you know the minute she contacts me again or if I find out anything. Okay?"

"Yes, I think that's a good idea. Frankly, if you don't find her in the next day or two, we need to consider getting help from the French authorities—assuming, of course, that that is where she is."

"Maybe you're right." There was another long pause and then Tillman said, "Mark, the phone calls I should return are stacking up. I need to get back to taking care of my clients. We will see you tomorrow at 10:00 a.m."

We ended our call and I buzzed Bryan.

"Chief, can I get back with you? We've had a system crash, and I'm up to my eyeballs trying to deal with it."

"Okay. Call me when you're ready."

"It may be late today or in the morning."

"Do what you have to do to keep us operational. Whatever you have will keep."

"Thanks, Chief." With that, Bryan clicked off.

My little gray cells were beginning to hurt. Paul Tillman was lying about those e-mails; I was sure of it. He either never received them or didn't want me to see them. But if he did receive them, they are still on his computer somewhere. Deleting something doesn't really make that something go away. Eventually some other data will overwrite the ones and zeros that constitute the digital form of the deleted information. Until then, people like those on Bryan's team, given enough time, can find and resurrect the ghostly image of that deleted information still inside the computer's memory. I intend to ask Bryan to do just that.

The same questions and the same possible answers were cycling through my mind. In short, I'm stuck in a rut. I decided the best thing to do was to give it a rest.

CHAPTER 23

Dashboard

If I was going to meet with the partners of the law firm, I needed to prepare, and it was a good way to rewire the gray cells. I needed to get out of the logic box that was limiting my perception. In short, I wanted to get out of the rut.

Law firms are unique commercial enterprises. They are not publicly owned so there is no separation between ownership and management as there is in a large corporation. But law firm partners don't just wear two hats, ownership and management. They wear them all. They are also the sales force. They have to bring in new business and hold on to the clients that they already have. That would be difficult enough, but there is one more hat, and it is the biggest one. They are the labor force—the means of production. They produce the product delivered to their customers. There aren't enough hours in the day to do justice to all four jobs—ownership, management, sales, and production.

The producer job always has priority. These people are trained as lawyers. They are lawyers because they want to practice law. They didn't go to law school to become salesmen or managers. Client work always comes first. If it didn't, fee revenues would dry up. Unhappy clients would go elsewhere, and inadequate attention would lead to malpractice claims and charges before the state bar. The jobs that suffer most are management first and sales second.

In all but the largest firms, there is often no one partner who is in charge. Every partner is an owner. Each has an equal voice and no one has absolute authority. Successful law firms are only accidentally successful, and it is easy for a law firm to be accidentally successful. Typical law firms generate $500,000 or more in fee revenue for every attorney in the firm and law firm partners share the 50% margin level.

The problem with being "accidentally successful" is that there can be a train wreck just around the corner, and no one sees it coming until it is too late. Law firms run on cash, and from the time a lawyer performs a service until the money for that service is collected is typically six months. A law firm can have a terrible fee generation month, and they would not feel its impact until six months later. That is when they would be surprised to find they didn't have money to meet their payroll or pay their suppliers for the goods and services needed to remain an operational business.

A bad month or several bad months can occur because a big case ends or one or more large clients leave the firm to go elsewhere. It can occur because of a downturn in the economy or the loss of billable personnel. The firm can have a large client who runs into financial trouble or files for bankruptcy.

Law firms can also spend their way to disaster. It takes time for new hires to become productive, and when they do, it takes an additional six months to fill their cash pipeline. Until then, the law firm is spending more to compensate its new associate than the cash the associate is generating. Hire too many people too fast and a law firm can grow itself into financial disaster.

In many ways, law firms are simple businesses. It is easy for them to succeed, but if no one is paying attention, they also fail easily! They don't survive adversity well.

Lawyers don't have time to read pages and pages of financial reports. And even if they did, they don't have the training to fully understand their implications. Traditional financial statements are not timely enough to head off pending train wrecks. Even if you have the skills to interpret the numbers, they only tell you what has already happened. They don't tell what is *likely* to happen. They don't tell what to do to head off a problem. In short, they don't give you information in time to change the outcome.

Instead of traditional financial reports, lawyers need a different approach. They need instantly digestible information—information that provides situational awareness so that the lawyer has an immediate sense of the law firm's financial performance against some measuring stick. What they don't need is a stack of computer reports at the end of each month. They don't have time to read them, and even if they did, it is too late to prevent whatever has already happened.

The answer is a "dashboard" just like the instrument panel or GPS system in an automobile. The instruments in an automobile tell you in real time how fast you're going and the direction of travel. They let you know when a door is ajar, a seatbelt isn't fastened, an engine needs servicing, or the air pressure in a tire is low. They monitor the battery, the cooling system, and the condition of the brakes. The GPS system lets you know that you missed a turn and how to get back on course. These navigation instruments tell you what you need to do to correct a pending problem before it is too late to do anything about it.

That is what Tillman and the other partners of his law firm need—a dashboard, a computerized instrument panel that provides a complete field of view over the business aspects of the law firm, something that gives them instant operational awareness. Luckily I had given a presentation on the benefits of dashboards a few months earlier. So in preparation for the meeting tomorrow, I copied the following example from that presentation to a PowerPoint slide.

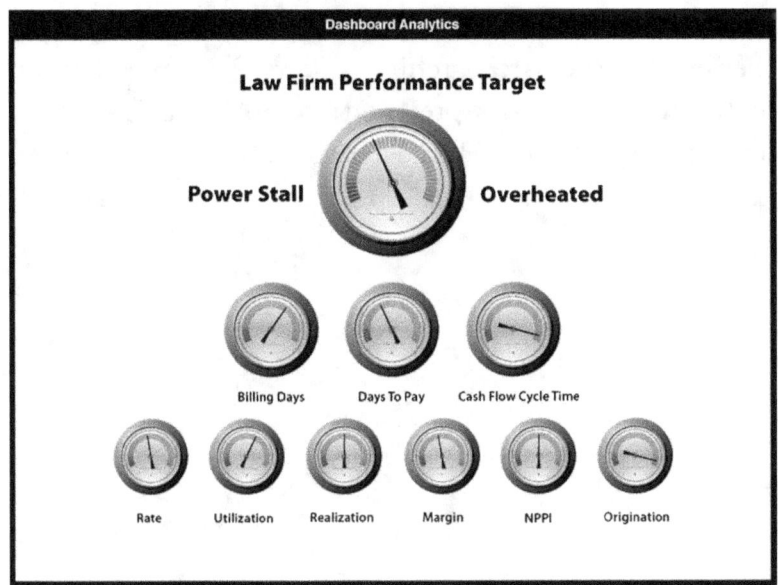

Dashboards, however, cannot be just a pretty picture. They must provide a drill-down conduit into the underlying information, and that capability has to answer the questions "why?" and "what can I do about it?" For example, the viewer can determine instantly if the firm is on target for billable hours worked this month. If not, the viewing partner can click on the dashboard gauge that tracks billable fees to quickly identify the attorney who has failed to submit their billable time to accounting. If accounting doesn't have the billable information, they can't bill it. Likewise, if the dashboard reflects a spike in billed but uncollected fees, the partner only has to click on that gauge to identify a client that failed to pay when expected and also the responsible attorney who needs to contact the client to collect the amount due.

When I meet with the partners on Monday, I don't want them to feel they are watching a PowerPoint presentation or listening to a sales presentation. So I decided to use only the one slide. That is really all that is needed. Lawyers are smart, and they are quick learners. They will get it.

CHAPTER 24

Friday Afternoon

The business week had flown by. I wasn't looking forward to the weekend. Weekends have their own sets of demands on one's time. I did not need the distraction of a two-day holiday. I was prepared for my business meeting with the partners, but the Lansden puzzle was still unsolved. I wanted to keep looking for pieces to the puzzle.

Before leaving for the day and giving in to the weekend, I decided to do a walkaround.

Shannon was all smiles as she said, "Mr. Rollins, I found a really nice furnished apartment at the Bristol on Broadway. It's a one bedroom with one-and-a-half baths. It's a condo owned by a medical school professor. He is renting it out because he is on sabbatical in Spain. The unit is available for immediate move-in, and the rent is just $1,095 per month. The condo building has everything, Mr. Rollins—an exercise room, a rooftop patio, and big garden area in the central core. It's a really nice place. Not your usual student pad, but it is within walking distance to the university."

"That is perfect, Shannon. You have made me a happy man. Call the rental agent and tell them to draw up the papers. Have them faxed to my home office. Unless some great disaster occurs, Dorin and Gabriela will be moving in this weekend.

I wasted no time. My cell phone was in hand, and I was calling Sarah. She answered, "Mark, I'm glad you called. I'm in the yard. It is a wonderful day, not too hot. There is a great breeze. The honeysuckle is in full bloom, and the sweet smell is delightful. I hope you come home in time to enjoy some of the day before it is all gone."

"I won't be long; I promise. But I'm going to make your day even better. I have found an apartment for Dorin and his wife. You can look it up on the Internet. It's a condo at the Bristol on Broadway, but it's being leased out by the owner. It's your job to break the news that we have decided to end their servitude and provide them with an apartment."

"What do I tell them? They will want to know why."

"Let's be honest. We made a commitment to them to provide room and board while Dorin is completing his studies. We have realized that we prefer our privacy so we're providing them with a fully-paid apartment near the university and a $200 a week food allowance."

"I hope it doesn't hurt Gabriela's feelings."

"You're a softy, Mrs. Rollins. The truth is I don't think they are going to be heartbroken. Show them the Internet pictures. They're going to love this place. And even if they don't—frankly, my dear, I don't give a damn."

Sarah chuckled, "Frankly, my dear, neither do I. I'll tell them to start packing."

"Tell Gabriela not to bother with dinner for us tonight. You and I are going to celebrate our freedom from domestics. I'll make a reservation at Criallo's. We'll start with a glass of Louis Roederer Cristal Champagne. I'll raid my Euro Cave for a 1964 Cheval Blanc. What do you say to all of that, M'lady?"

"I say it's a date!" Sarah's big smile could be heard over the phone.

Next, I called Tony. "Tony, I'm giving you a heads-up. We are going to move Dorin and Gabriela to an apartment this weekend. Don't make any plans unless you check with me first."

Tony laughed. "Okay, Mr. R., are you ready for me to pick you up?"

"In fifteen minutes. Also, I will need your chauffer services tonight. Sarah and I will be going out to dinner."

"Celebrating?"

"You got that right; I'll see you in fifteen."

I continued my walkaround. There are a lot of empty pieces of exercise equipment. That is unusual for Friday afternoon. I looked in on a few classes—Jazzercize®, yoga, and a spinning class. All three were less than half full.

I caught up with Meg on her way to sub for another missing instructor and asked, "What gives, Daughter? Where is everyone?"

"It's still the swine flu."

"I don't understand. According to the news this morning, there are only about 400 cases in the U.S., and so far, all of those cases appear to be mild."

"I should have said it is the swine flu *scare*. They have even shut down a couple of private schools. Our country's new Vice President didn't help things either. Did you hear what he said on one of the national news shows this morning?"

"No, what?"

"He said to avoid any place with a lot of people. Stay out of confined spaces like subway cars, trains, and elevators. He even said he would not fly on a commercial airplane! That is the kind of irresponsible talk going around now days. Dad, people are starting to stay home, and with all the talk, I can't blame them."

"The guy is a nutcase, Meg. He makes foolish comments all the time. The word 'Bidenism' has already worked its way into our vocabulary meaning foot-in-mouth disease."

"They say he's just being human."

"Do you really want the Vice President of the United States to be just another 'Joe'? I don't think so. The truth is I'm not sure if what he says or doesn't say makes any real difference because he is just one voice. The main reason people are frightened is because of the 24/7 sky-is-falling message on the news channels. Right now, the swine thing is being overhyped, but we do need to take reasonable precautions."

"Yes, Dad, and we are. We have wipes and hand sanitizers all over the place. The equipment is wiped down after every use. We're keeping everyone informed as well—as you and I discussed. If we actually have a case of the flu among our members or staff, we are prepared to close down for a few days."

"Good girl. I am heading home. Your mother and I are going out to dinner. Give us a call tomorrow, and maybe we can do something this weekend. The weather is supposed to be nice. We can cook out."

I went back to my office, googled for American flag pins, and ordered a hundred to give to people with a request that they, too, wear the pins upside down. What else can we do? Nothing, until a fresh new conservative leader surfaces. That needs to happen *soon*.

Shannon paged me, "Mr. Rollins, your car has arrived."

CHAPTER 25

Friday Night

Criallo's is less than ten minutes from our house. It is tucked in an unlikely out-of-the-way place in Franklin's Cool Springs—in a paddock building next door to a wine and spirits store. That friendly proximity makes for an exceptional wine list. Reviewers have described Criallo's as swanky. Out of the way or not, its cuisine and live music have attracted a loyal clientele that tend to be the smartly dressed, upwardly mobile crowd. Sarah and I usually raise the average age of their diners by a notch or two when we are there.

I spotted a Clams Casino appetizer. That is what I wanted but as the main course. The chef agreed to prepare an entrée-size dish of the clams for me. Sarah ordered a salmon dish. The champagne arrived. We clicked glasses and gave each other a wink.

Sarah took a sip of the champagne and asked, "Mark, have you heard any more about Amber Lansden? Her friends are worried about her."

"No—not much. They think she is somewhere in France. Sarah, I've been meaning to ask you about the Lansdens' marriage. Have you heard any talk that would suggest they were having problems?"

"Well, now that you ask, Helen Yoder did say that Amber had some strange mood swings lately. That is one of the reasons Helen is so concerned about Amber. She said that for about a year, Amber had been really down, and Helen was pretty sure it had to do with their marriage. But for the last three or four months, Amber had returned to her old self—upbeat and happy—until about a month ago when the gloom and doom came back. Helen said that Amber wouldn't tell her what was wrong. But when she visited Amber about a week before H.T.'s death, she picked up on the fact that H.T. and Amber now had separate bedrooms. I think that's a pretty good indication that things were not going well in the Lansden household. Don't you?"

"Yes, I would think so."

"All the marriage stuff aside, Mark, Helen and Amber have been close friends for years. Helen says that even when Amber was traveling, she always called. Helen hasn't heard from her since the memorial service—no phone calls, no e-mails, no postcards—nothing. According to Helen, that just isn't like her."

"I'm with Helen on this, Sarah. Something seems very wrong. I'm going to step up my efforts to find Amber."

"That's good. Have you found out anything more that sheds new light on H.T.'s awful death?"

"The more I investigate, the more questions I have. But I can tell you this ... I'm more convinced than ever that H.T. was murdered. I don't know why or who yet, but I'm going to find out. And, I'm going to make sure the people involved face the justice they deserve. H.T. was a good man, someone who was on track to make a difference in the world."

Our salads arrived, and we devoted the rest of the evening to plans for a family vacation on Hilton Head later in the year. We are renting a large house on the beach for the entire extended family.

Criallo's did an exceptional job as usual. I love Clams Casino. It's not a dish you usually find around Nashville. Criallo's clams were not perfect reproductions of the traditional Philadelphia and southern New Jersey dishes, but they were close enough to make me a happy camper.

We made it home by 9:00 p.m. While still in the restaurant, I had received two separate text messages on my BlackBerry. One was from Bryan and the other from Mariko. Both requested that I call them. Sarah knew it probably related to the H.T. situation, and she is as committed as I am to get to the bottom of things. With her blessings, I headed to my home office. Bryan would still be at the WH Club.

He answered quickly, "Glad you called, Chief. I wanted to finish giving you my report before I called it a night."

"Did you take care of the system crash?"

"Yes, we are back to normal. If you recall when we entered the agreement with Homeland Security to provide a covert search and database capability, we started mirroring everything to a remote server in Iron Mountain. So except for the technical guys who were working to reestablish normal fail-safe mode, no one was affected. No one outside our group had any idea that we had an anomaly."

"Good, let's get back to your investigative work. What have you found out about Santo?"

"Mariko's instinct about Owen Santo appears well grounded. The guy is single and pulls down a decent salary—$65,000. But, he is living a more expensive life than $65,000 will pay for. He has a penthouse condo in one of the new Nashville high-rises. The price was $875,000; he paid $175,000 up front and financed the remaining $700,000. He purchased it unfurnished. I found traffic on Facebook that references his decorating skills. The furnishings are rumored to be expensive and first class. He appears to have paid for those purchases outright—no indication of installment purchases.

He charges ten to fifteen thousand a month on his credit cards but pays in full at the end of the month. He commutes to work in a Toyota Prius, but has a $95,000 Jaguar XK convertible that he drives after hours. He has accounts at Bank of America and one of the small independent banks. You add them together, and we are talking about almost $250,000 in low yield money market and interest bearing checking accounts. I searched in the usual places and didn't come up with any investment accounts. There is no apparent source of income other than his salary from the law firm."

"It sounds like Mr. Santo is supplementing his income big time."

"Chief, if all this supplemental income is coming from the law firm, wouldn't you think someone would notice? We're not talking about chump change here."

"Maybe someone did."

"You mean like Mr. Lansden?"

"Actually, that could be what H.T. wanted to talk to me about."

Bryan continued, "Good point. Let me give you a little more on his lifestyle. According to his credit card receipts, he is a regular in lower Broad and Second Avenue hangouts and nightclubs. From the size of some of the charges, it looks to me like he is quick to pick up the tab—plays the big shot role probably as a pickup technique. If we are to believe his Facebook profile, he hangs with the up-and-coming Nashville entertainment crowd. He has lots of pictures on Facebook. My take on the pictures is that he works the female tourist types—has them thinking he is their introduction to their favorite Nashville star.

The condo maintains a log of unaccompanied guests arriving to visit a particular resident. The condo owner has to approve their entrance. Santo does have two repeat visitors, one female and one male. The female is a regular, like clockwork, once a month—the 26th, 27th, or 28th. She is Miss Rachel Pappas, a stripper who works one of the clubs in the Alley. The male is another employee at the law firm, Bill Maxwell."

"Bill Maxwell, you say, very interesting ... so the two are friends!"

"Right. They are about the same age and Facebook pictures have them partying together."

"Bryan, have you found anything that would indicate the guy is capable of murder—any history of violence? How about any criminal record?"

"Except for a DUI almost ten years ago, the guy appears clean. I do need to tell you that he is a registered gun owner. He purchased a gun last year from a Nashville gun dealer. It is practically a bazooka. It's a full size .45 manufactured by National."

"Does he have a carry permit?"

"No, however, in Tennessee it isn't necessary to have a carry permit to purchase a handgun. Without the permit, you cannot transport a loaded handgun. You can have it at home for personal protection. You can transport the weapon as long as it is unloaded and secured."

"The .45 caliber would be consistent with the muzzle flash and loud report noted by the witnesses, but it's an automatic. That doesn't fit with the missing shell casings at the scene. And we know that the caliber of weapon that killed H.T. was a .25, not a .45."

"I agree, Chief. I need to tell you, however, that we did find a firm-related handgun registration that does match up with the caliber of the bullet that killed him."

"Whose?"

"Amber Lansden. She is the registered owner of a .25 Beretta Modelo 418."

* * *

Mariko was obviously waiting for my call. She answered before the first ring was complete, "Hello, Boss."

"Sorry to call so late. What have you got for me?"

"A new player showed up on my radar screen today— an associate lawyer, William Maxwell. They call him Bill. Spends a lot of time in Santo's office. He was waiting in Santo's office when I arrived this morning. Santo didn't seem very happy to see him when he arrived about 15 minutes behind me. They spent almost two hours behind closed doors. The top half of the wall of Santo's office is glass. I couldn't hear what they were talking about, but there were no smiles or laughs. Whatever was going on between them, it must have been *serious* stuff."

I filled in Mariko on what we know about Bill Maxwell including his frequent visits to Santo's apartment, his resignation, and that he picked up the package sent by Hudson Bluff Mortgage to Lansden's mailbox in Spring Hill. Mariko agreed to do some probing among the accounting staff to discover the exact nature of the connection between Santo and Maxwell. Are they just friends, or is there more to the relationship? Then we shifted our attention to concentrate on Santo himself.

"Mariko, he is clearly living beyond his salary level. We need to know for sure how Santo is getting that additional money."

"Boss, today is the 25th of the month. That's when the law firm distributes payroll checks. So yesterday, that was what Carolyn Osburn and I worked on. We processed the payroll and printed checks so that they would be ready for Santo to hand out today. It made me think of something in one of the fraud case studies at Vanderbilt. It involved the use of phantom employees to embezzle funds. We should compare the payroll with the law firm's employee roster."

"Good idea. Can you get a copy of the payroll register?"

"I can try, but wouldn't it be easier to have Bryan hack into the law firm's computer system?"

"Mariko, we need to start thinking about evidence that can be used by the authorities. When we hack into the computer system of a commercial enterprise, we also happen to break a few laws. So it would be better if you, as an employee of the law firm, obtained the copy."

"Okay. I'll give it a try."

"Mariko, I also think the time has come to get our hands on those old bank statements. Plan to leave something 'absentmindedly,' maybe your cell phone, in the office when you leave on Monday. That will give you an excuse to return after everyone has gone for the day. You need some alone time inside the office so you can locate where they file their old bank statements and cancelled checks. Get at least the last three months for us to check."

"Sounds like a plan, Boss. On another subject, do you want to know what I was able to find out from Carolyn Osburn about the firm's compensation plan?"

"Absolutely, Mariko. I gathered some info from my discussions with Tillman. Let's see if it matches with what you have learned."

"Boss, it seems that every attorney has the same base salary. The exception is new hires, of course. They work up to the standard base after they have been in the firm for three years. Everyone, partners and associates, are on an equal footing after their initial three years. In addition to the base, each receives 20% of the fees collected from clients that they bring into the firm—and that is for life."

"Mariko, that's consistent with what I have been able to find out. However, I also got a little clarification from Tillman about the 'for life' part. It is for life but only as long as the individual remains in the firm. If the lawyer retires or goes into public service, I understand there is a seven-year buyout plan. And all payments stop upon death."

"That's right, Boss. I also learned what happens to the 20% that would have been paid to the dead attorney. Those origination fees go into a pot they refer to as the House Account. The pot is shared equally by the remaining partners. Until now, what has been in the House Account has been insignificant. H.T.'s death changes everything. He was the biggest rainmaker. His origination fees, the 20% that he received every year, were more than the origination fees earned by everyone else in the law firm *combined*. With him dead, there is now a big difference between partner compensation and the non-partner senior associates due to the sharing of that House Account. Until his death, the difference in income between individual lawyers in the firm was almost entirely due to each attorney's ability to bring in new business. He who brought in the most business made the most money."

"That's good intel, Mariko. The House Account is not the only windfall created by H.T.'s death. Do you know about the insurance policy?"

"Yes, I do—ten million that pays double if Lansden's death was accidental. The three remaining partners of the law firm are profiting greatly from H.T.'s untimely death."

"Right you are, Mariko. It is enough joint motive to make me think about *Murder on the Orient Express*. All of them had a damn good reason to want the man dead!"

CHAPTER 26

Another Phone Conversation

"George and Devora Small were in the office yesterday. Mrs. Small saw that Mariko woman in the hall. She asked me about her. She was quite surprised when I told her she was working in our accounting department. Mrs. Small ran off at the mouth for thirty minutes about Mariko and some fitness club in Brentwood. If you believe her, this Rollins person is some super sleuth, and Mariko is his Dr. Watson. She kept talking about what she called the 'Rollins' Adventures'. Is this Mariko a plant? Do you think she's spying on us?"

"I don't think so. I know she worked at that fitness club but started there while she was going to Vanderbilt. She was an instructor. That's not the kind of job for someone with an MBA. That's why she took our job."

"I don't like it. I don't like it at all."

"Stay calm; everything will play out the way we want it."

"Now, this Rollins guy is going to attend the partners' meeting, and we have a damn homicide detective who has set up shop in Conference Room Four. Feels like things are coming apart—closing in on us."

"Nonsense. Rollins is just a software guy who made a lot of money. He knows a lot about law firm management. That's it. He's not some super hero!"

"What about Amber? Have you taken care of that?"

"It's being taken care of as we speak."

"She is bad news. We should have left her out of this."

"Look, it was *her* idea. I didn't know she couldn't handle it. I got her on Valium after the memorial service."

"She is still a big risk. And your solution could turn out to make things worse."

"Just chill out, man! We didn't have a choice. You know that; and if you start acting guilty, *you'll* be the problem."

"You can say 'chill out,' but *you* didn't pull the trigger!"

"As far as the law is concerned, I might as well have. But I have a backup plan if we have to use it. One that will put us in the clear even if the drunk shooter story doesn't hold up."

"I want to hear it."

"We hang H.T.'s death on someone else."

"If the story about the drunk stops working, the police will know two people were involved."

"Right—and I know just the two people to hang this on."

"I was *crazy* to let you talk me into this."

"*Bull shit*! You needed the money; that's why you're in this. We are in it together, and the only way for you to come out of this okay is for you to listen to me and do exactly what I tell you to do."

"Yeah, you got me by the balls."

"Alright, do you still have Amber's little Beretta?"

"Yes, of course."

"I want you to bring it to me. It will be our get-out-jail-free card."

"You will use it to frame the other two?"

"Yes. Of course, they will need to be in no condition to claim their innocence."

"Shit! How many damn people are you prepared to get rid of?"

"As many as we have to."

"While you are at it, what about this Mariko and Rollins?"

"If what Mrs. Small told you is even partly true, you can bet Rollins has some serious enemies. I think I'll start looking for them."

"Now, that I like."

"Okay, are we done for now?"

"Yes. I'll deliver the gun to you."

CHAPTER 27

Amber Lansden

Breakfast was great. No Gabriela—just Sarah and me along with cereal, bananas, and raisins. Alone at last! Cheerios for me and some healthy sawdust-like stuff for Sarah. We were enjoying our breakfast on the screened porch. The temperature was a perfect 70 degrees. The air smelled of honeysuckle. The birds were industrious. Blue birds were going in and out of the houses I installed on the picket fence around the garden area close to the house. Robins and cardinals were harvesting pine straw for their spring nests' construction sites.

I had asked Tony to bring the car around at 9:00 a.m. I didn't want to be late for my meeting with the partners. Nine o'clock came quickly. I gave by favorite lady a kiss and joined Tony for the drive to Nashville's center city. We were just passing the Brentwood Exit when the navigation system indicated an incoming call. I answered. The voice on the other end was excited, but not in a good way.

"Mark, this is Paul Tillman."

"Yes, Paul, what's up?"

"It's Amber!" he said in a choking voice.

"You have located her?"

"She's dead—*murdered*!" he gasped.

"Paul, you need to take a deep breath. I need you to fill me in on everything you know."

"I don't have all the details yet. We got a call this morning. Our receptionist put it through to me."

"Who called?"

"The *gendarmerie* found her. I got a call from the investigating magistrate. According to the magistrate, it appears she was killed in the course of a robbery."

"How was she killed?"

"He said strangulation. I think she was found in some cheap hotel outside the city of Bordeaux."

"Shit" was all I could think of at first. Then I asked, "Is that where she has been all this time?"

"No, the French authorities said she was registered at the Grand Barrail Château in St. Emilion. She had gone to Bordeaux that night to the Place de la Victoire. My French is not very good, and the investigator spoke English with a heavy accent. If I understood him correctly, this is an area with lots of bars and restaurants. Apparently, she either went willingly to the hotel with someone or was forced. Her money and credit cards were missing. She was roughed up pretty bad."

I wasn't sure I liked Amber, but I damn well didn't like the mental image of her badly beaten and strangled body that flashed in my head. Nor did I like the guilt I was feeling for not pressing Paul to go to the authorities to help find her. I could have stopped this from happening.

"Do you have the name of the magistrate?" Maybe I could still help.

"Yes, Andrè Delorme. He is in Bordeaux."

"Can you send me his contact information?"

"I have his phone number. I'll send you that. Mark, you can forget about our meeting this morning. We have to deal with this."

"I understand. We can reschedule later."

"I don't know. I don't think I have the heart for that anymore." Paul Tillman hung up his phone.

I knew what I had to do next. I called Sam Littleton. "Sam, it's Mark Rollins. Have you talked to McGovern yet?"

"Yes, he is okay with a get-together whenever you want to do it."

"Right now—today! Amber Lansden has been murdered. If her death is unrelated to H.T.'s, then it would be a bizarre coincidence—and I don't believe in coincidences!"

"Where and when do you want to meet?"

"My place—as soon as possible. I would like to have my team there. Square it with McGovern. Everyone has a piece of this puzzle. We need to pull it all together before someone else is killed."

"Do you think there is a danger of that?"

"I didn't think Amber was in danger. But I was wrong. I am convinced that there is more than one person involved in whatever is afoot. Killers know there is one sure way to keep their co-conspirators from hanging them. They know dead men don't talk. We may have a killer on track to eliminate anyone who is a risk to him."

"Okay, it's 9:30 a.m.; I'll get McGovern to your place by 11:30. Will that work?"

"Yes. I'll supply lunch and, if necessary, dinner and breakfast. Let's do whatever it takes to bring this guy down. Do you have a contact in INTERPOL who can act as liaison between us and the French *gendarmerie?*"

"So we are dealing with the military police?"

"Yes, as you know the French military is the law enforcement authority for rural areas and small villages. Apparently, they found her body in one of those low cost hotels in the countryside."

"That is in our favor, Mark. From the FBI's standpoint, they are easier for us to work with than the police in the cities."

* * *

Tony took the Demonbreun Street Exit and then reentered the interstate reversing our course. We headed back toward Brentwood. I had one more call I needed to make.

Sarah's answer was cheerful, "Hello, Husband. You are really missing out on another gorgeous day."

"The day is not that gorgeous on my end. Amber Lansden is dead, apparently murdered."

"Oh, NO! That's terrible! I really need to talk to Helen Yoder. Can I tell her before she hears it on the news?"

"Yes, that's why I'm calling. I can't give you details right now. I'll try to do that when I have more reliable information. Okay?"

"I understand. I'm just trying to think. Did she have any brothers or sisters? What about the parents—are they still living? There are probably other people I should contact."

"I don't know, Sarah. I'll leave that up to you. Maybe Helen knows."

"Yes, she and I will talk about that."

"I have to go now, Sarah."

"Wait! There is something I need to tell you."

"What is it?"

"After we had dinner the other night, I talked to Helen again about Amber. After learning about the separate bedrooms, Helen confronted her. Amber admitted that H.T. had threatened to divorce her. Apparently, he had discovered she had, or was having, an affair. Helen doesn't know who it was with, but Amber did tell her that he was married."

"That clears some things up for me; I'm glad you followed up with Helen."

"Me too, but it is sad. Mark, please call and tell me more of the details as soon as you can."

"I will."

CHAPTER 28

Face-Off

"Detective McGovern, I didn't realize you were still here."

"I just have a few things I need to clear up, Mr. Tillman. I hope you can spare me a few minutes of your time."

"Detective, this isn't a good time. We just received word that Mrs. Lansden was killed in France—murdered, they think."

"Yes, I know. Strange coincidence, don't you think?"

"No, I don't, Detective. This can't have anything to do with H.T.'s death. She was halfway around the world."

"All the same, Mr. Tillman, consider the odds. For every 100,000 people in this country, there are only four murders. In France, it is less than 2 out of 100,000. We have a situation here where both husband and wife, thousands of miles apart, are murdered within weeks of each other. The odds of that happening are in the stratosphere. You'd have better odds winning the lottery."

"You have been a detective too long, McGovern. In the first place, I don't agree with you that H.T. was murdered. It was an accident. It wasn't murder! I might add that the insurance company agrees with me. They wired the insurance proceeds to the firm this morning."

"The full $20 million?"

"Well, no; we agreed on a $17 million settlement."

"So the insurance company wasn't 100% in your camp on this accident thing."

"Yes, they were, Detective! The only dispute was over the double indemnity question. Was it the type of accident that qualifies for a doubling of the coverage? They agreed that there was no intent on the drunk's part to kill H.T. His death was simply the result of some drunk's reckless behavior."

"Well, then we have something we agree on, Mr. Tillman."

"How so?"

"The drunk didn't intend to kill H.T. The fact is we are pretty sure that H.T. was killed by someone other than your drunk."

"Ridiculous—everyone in the Alley that night saw what happened," Tillman sputtered.

"I think there were two people and two different guns. One gun that killed Lansden and one gun fired in the air by your drunk as a diversion. And, I have reason to believe that one of those two guns was yours."

"*My* gun?"

"Yes. And Mr. Tillman, let me remind you that your whereabouts at the time of H.T.'s death is still a question mark."

"The hell it is! I told you I was on my way home. Are you calling me a liar?"

"I am simply pointing out that as a detective I have reason to believe that your gun was involved in the death of your law partner and that your whereabouts at the time of his death has not yet been verified. You are not a suspect, but you have not been eliminated as a *possible* suspect. That's why I'm here this morning, Mr. Tillman. Let's see if I can eliminate you. Shall we?"

"I should throw you out of my office. We have just had our second terrible tragedy. Where is your compassion? Let me make this clear, McGovern. I'll answer your questions this morning, but I don't want you on the premises for the rest of the day. I will not tolerate your continued lack of consideration for the feelings of the people in this law firm."

"Mr. Tillman, if you hamper my investigation, I will arrest you for obstruction of justice. My compassion is for the murder victims, and I intend to put someone in jail for those crimes. Now, you can either tolerate my presence, or I will haul your people downtown, one person at a time."

To McGovern it seemed like the temperature of the room was rising. It was now a stand-off—a game of wills. He who spoke first would lose. McGovern's eyes remained locked on the attorney's, holding his ground against the weight of Tillman's intense stare. In a standoff, seconds can seem like minutes, minutes like hours. McGovern had no intention of yielding. He counted in silence, a trick he had learned from an old cop, "One Mississippi, two Mississippi, three Mississippi, four Mississippi, five Mississippi, six Mississippi, seven Mississippi, eight Mississippi, nine Mississippi...."

Tillman had no gimmick to rely on and no alternative but to relent. He broke the silence. He lost. "Let's get this over with, McGovern. Ask me what you will—but make it *damn* fast!"

"Alright, I'll be fast, providing you give me fast answers. You said that you had never fired your handgun—that it was still loaded with the same old bullets that were in the gun at the time you received it from your father?"

"That is right!"

"Has the handgun been fired by anyone else?"

"Of course not!"

"How do you explain the fact that when we tested the gun we found copper deposits not lead deposits in the barrel of the pistol?"

"What the hell does that mean?"

"It means to me that someone removed the old lead bullets, reloaded the handgun with new copper-clad cartridges, fired the weapon until it was empty, and then reloaded the pistol with the original lead bullets."

"I don't know anything about that. You saw where I kept the handgun. Anyone could take it out of my desk."

"Do you know if anyone ever did that?"

"Well, uh, yes—maybe Owen. Now I remember. I told him about the gun because he often works late. I told him that he could take the gun to his office on those nights that he worked late."

"Did he do that?"

"I don't know. I told him he could, but I never asked him if he had taken me up on my offer."

"Anyone else?"

"Not that I know of. But, I've never kept the gun a secret. Someone else could have taken it."

"Did you know that your security system has Bill Maxwell entering or reentering the building at 10:05 p.m.? That would have been right after the reported shooting."

"No, I didn't know. But that doesn't mean anything. Maybe he went out to buy something to eat. We all do that when working late. The Arcade is only minutes away. Have you asked him about it?"

"He claimed it wasn't him. He said he lost his pass card months ago and got a replacement. Maybe someone found the original card and used it. When I pressed him for an alibi, he started to clam up. He didn't want to answer any more questions without an attorney."

"That is his right."

"Did he know about your gun?"

"He could have. I don't know. What about fingerprints?"

"Curious... there weren't any."

"Oh."

"Yeah, Mr. Tillman. Someone wiped the gun and the shell casings clean."

"Detective, do you still have my gun?"

"Yes, and we are going to keep it for a while."

CHAPTER 29

Cornerman

The man on the corner of Lafayette and Lewis streets is the godfather of his little intersection of sidewalks. If you are buying, he is selling or taking a cut to arrange what you are looking for. He won his turf the hard way, by fighting for it. He keeps it by taking on anyone who tries to cut into his business. He carries a Beretta TomCat .32 loaded with hollow points. By the age of 17, he had already killed three men.

Today the cornerman is wearing a red tank top. His jeans are loose and beltless in mimic of brothers who have done time. His running shoes are Karhu M1s. The cornerman stared suspiciously at the well dressed man and asked, "You kinda slummin', ain't you?"

"Yes, I'm in the market for something."

"You cattin' off? Why else would you be in my hood, man? What I'm sellin', you don't find where *you* live. That right?"

"I'm not looking for drugs."

"Alright, man. I got girls."

"That's not it either. What I want is worth more to you—I'm talking *big* money."

"How big?"

"Say $5,000."

"What you thinkin', man? That's chump change. Get you enough blow or smoke to go into business, or I'll sell you some bitches. That's all $5,000 gets you, man."

"What if I were talking about more money?"

"Muthafucka! You wanna *ice* somebody!"

"What?"

"You know, man… You wanna rub somebody out—cap 'em—right?"

"Right, I want someone eliminated."

"The money depends, man. If it's easy, know what I mean, 10 grand make it happen."

"What if it isn't easy?"

"Not in th' *hard* business, man, but for a price, I'll hook ya up."

"How do I know you won't just be taking my money?"

"Yo, man, this is my corner. I'm a businessman. I don't deliver… you know where to find me. Know what I'm sayin'?"

"I'll give you $1,000 if you introduce me to the right person."

"Now it's *my* turn, man. You some white ass big shot but *I don't know you!* B'for I deliver, I gotta know you'll hand over my commission."

"Why would I want to screw you? Here's $500. I'll give you the other five when you introduce me to the man I need to do business with."

"Sweet—brand new Benjamins. You come back in two hours, whitie. Man you lookin' for will be here."

CHAPTER 30

Case Room

Bryan had converted the largest of the WH Club's conference rooms into a case room. It would stay that way until the H.T. Lansden matter was closed, one way or the other. The room is equipped with video conferencing and high-speed access to the Internet. Electronic whiteboards digitally capture anything written on them into a central database that also contains all other case-related information and images.

To facilitate communication among the members of the case room team, Bryan supplied each member with a Nikto—a small but powerful communicator. The new device is about the size of an iPod with a detachable earpiece that fits into a slot molded into the case. When worn, the earpiece is surprisingly comfortable and virtually invisible. The earpiece also serves as a microphone and will even pick up the wearer's whispers. When the earpiece is returned to the case, the unit performs like a cross between a cell phone and a walkie-talkie. An incoming call will cause the unit to vibrate when in stealth mode or emit a ringtone when in normal mode. Once the call is answered, the connection remains open for two-way style communication. To initiate an outgoing call, the unit responds to voice commands. All you have to do to call an individual in the group is to touch the earpiece and say, "Nikto Call." Then speak the first or last name of the person with whom you want to communicate. "Nikto Call Conference" will instantly open a connection to every member of the group simultaneously. Bryan would act as "Control Central" for the group.

The Nikto communicators also included one additional capability. Built into each unit are two small removable GPS tracking devices about the size of a medicine capsule. Either capsule can be covertly placed on another person, such as a suspect, to track that individual's movements. A capsule can also be swallowed if you are in danger and want to be sure that the Control Center can track your whereabouts if the communicator is destroyed or taken from you.

By 11:30 a.m., everyone was in place. Sam Littleton, head of the regional FBI office; Parker McGovern, Metro homicide detective; Tony Caruso, my driver and bodyguard; Bryan Gray, the WH Club's CIO or, as I prefer to call him, the brain trust leader; and Mariko Lee, VP of Security for the Club. Parker McGovern was clearly uncomfortable and unhappy. Sam tried his best to make him understand that we were not ordinary butt-in types. The WH Club brain trust is something akin to the A-Team or the Mission

Impossible team, except that most of the time we limit our scope of operation to the cyber world. We can go where official police and government bodies can't, and we are paid well to do just that. While cyberspace is our normal field of operation, Mariko, Tony, and I can hold our own on terra firma against the toughest bad guys.

In the H.T. Lansden case, we were acting on our own, however. No government agency was paying us or giving us cover. We were strictly civilians. McGovern was an old school cop who guards his turf even when dealing with other official investigative bodies. When it comes to civilians, he has a visceral dislike for anyone meddling in his investigations. I needed to give him something worthwhile to win him over to our little team. He was, however, rather in awe of the technology on display in the case room.

"Detective McGovern, thank you for agreeing to meet with us. I believe Sam has filled you in on our rather unique capabilities."

"Look, Mr. Rollins, I'm here only because Sam Littleton asked me to be here. If you or your people have information pertinent to this murder case, you need to turn it over to me now. I don't need to tell you that your failure to do so would be serious. If I determine that you are withholding information, I will not hesitate to arrest you for obstruction of justice. I want to be very clear that my being here doesn't mean I necessarily intend to share any information with you. And, if I should decide to provide you with any of my findings, I reserve the right to hold back anything I so chose."

"Very good, Detective; we know where you stand. I am pleased, however, to hear you refer to H.T.'s death as murder. We have no doubt about that whatsoever. We will give you everything we have. I ask you to keep in mind that we have an extraordinary talent for finding the answers—if we know the questions. It is your unanswered questions in which I'm most interested. Tell us what they are, and let us find the answers for you. Let me start our meeting by summarizing what we know about the events surrounding Lansden's death....

The map on the display shows the position of our victim's body where it fell in Printers Alley. H.T. worked late the night he died, leaving the office shortly before 10:00 p.m. At approximately 10:00 p.m., witnesses reported observing an apparently intoxicated male near the intersection of Printers Alley and Bankers Alley.

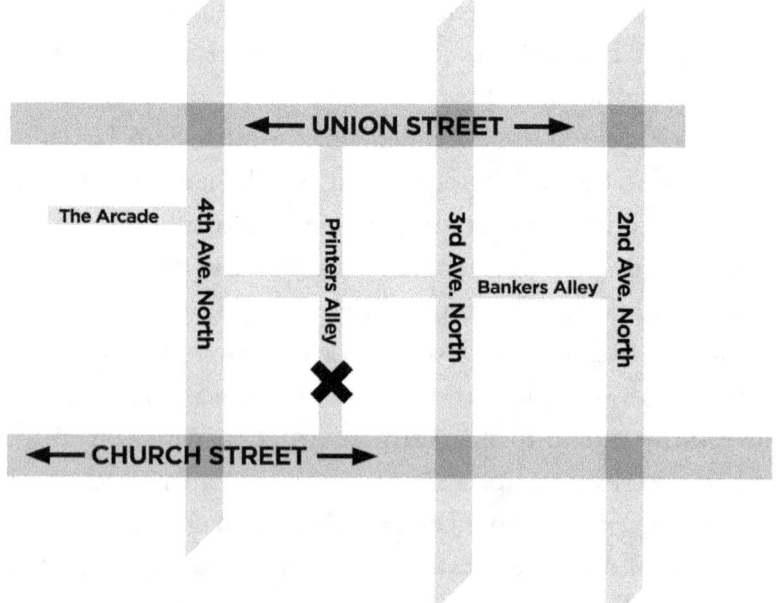

This person was wildly firing a handgun skyward in celebratory fashion. According to witnesses, the shooter wore jeans, a sports jacket of some kind, and a cowboy hat.

Since Printers Alley is near the heavily trafficked Second Avenue tourist area and is a tourist attraction on its own, police had the area closed off almost immediately. There were lots of people in jeans and cowboy hats, but none who appeared extremely inebriated or bore any evidence of having fired a weapon.

Did I miss anything, Detective?"

"So far, you got it right."

"What the police found was a very dead Harold T. Lansden. As shown on the displayed map of Printers Alley, his body was located about midway down the block between the Church Street entrance and Bankers Alley, the reported location of the shooter. The initial assumption was that one of the stray bullets of the intoxicated shooter killed Lansden.

According to the autopsy report, Lansden was killed by a single .25 caliber shot to the head. The angle of the entry was straight on to the side of the head. The entry angle and the slight powder burns present were not consistent with the stray bullet scenario. At the same time, the small amount of powder burns was too light for a straight-on point-blank gunshot. The autopsy report also noted a microscopic amount of material in the wound which would be consistent with the firing of a weapon from inside of a concealment device such as a purse or jacket. This would also explain the lower-than-expected powder burn evidence."

"How about it, Detective? Did I miss anything important as far as the autopsy report is concerned?"

"No, but the fact that you have that information concerns the hell out of me. Those findings have not been released to the public. They are part of an ongoing police investigation, and damn it, I want to know who leaked them to you."

"As I told you, Detective, we have an unusual ability to find answers to questions, and we seldom have to depend on leaks. No information stored in a computer is beyond our ability to access it."

"The hell it isn't—at least legally! If you are breaking into police systems, you are committing a *goddamn felony*."

"That may be, Detective. But, note that you don't see Sam raising the issue. That's because we have a special license (call it forgiveness) based on our relationship with a number of government agencies who take advantage of our unique talents and who know from experience that we do not misuse the information we access."

McGovern, looking disgruntled, didn't say anything for several seconds. He looked at Littleton who had made no effort to counter or modify my statement about a special license. Then he said, "Rollins, this just doesn't sound kosher to me, but I will leave it for now. Go on with your story."

"We know that you did not find any spent shell casings at the scene. And, we know that the witnesses commented on the bright muzzle flash and loud report of the shooter's handgun. Those facts point to a large-caliber revolver. Thus Lansden must have been murdered by a second weapon, a .25 automatic fired from a concealment device. The need to conceal the weapon means that Lansden probably knew his killer. Lansden, like others in the Alley, had his attention drawn to the intoxicated shooter who was acting as a diversion. An accomplice then shot Lansden."

Tony said, "What I don't understand, Mr. R., is why the witnesses didn't report hearing the second gun—the .25 caliber."

"It is an alley, Tony, with buildings on both sides. There would have been a lot of echo. Even if the killer hadn't timed his shot perfectly, the muffled sound of the small caliber weapon from inside the concealment device would have blended in with the reverberating echoes."

"That's the way we see it," said the detective. "We have identified the source of the material in the wound. The concealment device, as you referred to it, was a leather envelope-style portfolio by Royce®. The victim's law firm gives them to their upscale clients."

"So, Detective McGovern, while it doesn't follow with certainty, the killer was in all probability a member of the law firm or a client. You agree?"

"It is a useful assumption for now, and that is the direction where we are concentrating. Look Rollins, before we go any further with the *Detective McGovern* thing, why don't we make this easier? Just call me Parker."

"Okay, Parker. And, we're okay with first names all the way around."

"Mark, you want questions. Well, one thing has been bugging me—why didn't we find the so-called drunk shooter? I think we can conclude that the shooter was putting on an act, but what happened to him? My department was all over that place in seconds. The exits were closed, and we ID'd and questioned everyone leaving the Alley that night—even field-tested their hands for gunpowder residue using the new GSPR test kit. It's a spray test."

"Are you sure you checked everyone, Parker? Weren't you looking for a man? Maybe your actor wasn't a male. When you say your department ID'd and tested everyone, did that include women leaving the area?"

The detective paused before answering. "No, dammit, we didn't. A woman could have walked out of the place with a shopping bag or one of those big tote-bag purses with the hat and jacket inside. We wouldn't have stopped her. And we didn't collect bystander's names unless they said they witnessed the events. Damn," Parker said in frustration.

It was Bryan who spoke next. "Chief, I think I have something that would be of interest in that regard."

"What is that, Bryan?"

"We ran background checks on everyone connected to the case. Amber Lansden was Amber Price before her marriage. She attended, but did not graduate from, an upscale all-women's college in western New York. The one area she apparently excelled in was drama. She was in several plays performed at the college. What is unique about those performances is that women play all the parts—male and female. Here is the kicker. She had a leading role in Eugene O'Neill's *A Moon for the Misbegotten*. She played James Tyrone, an alcoholic. I might add she got rave reviews for her believable performance of his more drunken moments."

I said, "That could explain a lot."

Detective McGovern asked, "What about motive?"

"Parker, I assume you know about the insurance policy?"

"Yes, you think this was about that?"

"I do. I don't have any hard evidence, but I have reason to believe that H.T. Lansden was about to divorce his wife for having an affair. She would have been humiliated and penniless. If not literally penniless, certainly penniless compared to the lifestyle she had become accustomed to."

"Okay, that is another question. How do we get the hard evidence?"

Bryan exclaimed, "The lockbox!"

Detective McGovern faced Bryan and asked, "What lockbox?"

I stepped in saying, "That's another chapter in this story. I really need to back up and give you some background information before answering that question. Let's take a 30-minute break. We have ordered lunch. It's set up right outside."

CHAPTER 31

Meeting Continues

When we got back together, Detective Parker McGovern had crossed over to our side completely. After I filled him in on the Hudson Bluff Mortgage aspects of the case, he said, "Mark, this is a completely new angle for Metro. We knew none of this. Let me summarize to make sure I got it down:

- The two players at Hudson are the CEO, Keith Nelson, and the CFO, one Gordon Seemann;
- Someone unknown in the law firm provided the Hudson CFO with the Fenio case file;
- Seemann sent a package to this 'unknown' person; however, attorney Bill Maxwell picked it up.

Is that about it, Mark?"

Mariko was late getting back to the case room following our lunch break. She was walking into the meeting just as I said, "Yes, Parker. You have the key facts right, but there are several unanswered questions. My first unanswered question is: what was in the package?"

Mariko had taken advantage of the break to change her clothes. She had ditched the conservative apparel she had worn as an accounting assistant and replaced it with something that was more Mariko. She was wearing a black Anatomie sleeveless tank jacket top from Deezfit with a mock turtleneck. The low-rise boot-cut pants were black as well. She was also carrying a small purse, mail-pouch-like, that was riding on her right hip from a long strap that crossed from her left shoulder. I had no doubt about the contents of that purse. It held Mariko's new handgun, a 9mm Springfield EMP®.

Mariko had not given up on her Beretta Vertec; she had simply added the new Springfield to her personal armory. The Vertec, designed for the smaller hands of a woman, is a slimmed-down version of Beretta's model 92, but it is still a two-pound weapon. The EMP, 10 ounces lighter, has the same kill power, and its classic 1911 profile still commands plenty of respect from anyone on the muzzle end of the gun. The EMP's small size and big power are the attributes you want in a concealed weapon.

Mariko returned to the chair across from Parker McGovern and sat down. She took off the purse and put it on the conference table. Most people wouldn't have noticed, but the purse made the sound of a weighted object as Mariko placed it on the table. McGovern did notice, and he recognized the slight smell of gunpowder. The pistol had been fired recently—probably at a firing range. The detective looked questioningly at Mariko. He took in the full measure of her.

She smiled at him and said, "It's okay Parker; I'm VP of Security. I'm licensed, and I'm ex-military—Marine MP."

"You got to be kidding! You, a small thing, a cop, *and* a Marine at that?"

I said, "Parker, don't let the small package fool you. She is a black belt, too. As they say, she can kill you 23 different ways with just her hands."

"Okay! Okay! I believe you. We have Marines and MPs in Metro, and they are tough as nails. Look, lady, once a cop always a cop. I'm glad to have you on my team. In fact, if you ever decide to get back in the cop business, I would love to have you in my car. It would make coming to work a real pleasure."

I was surprised that McGovern was able to say that without sounding lecherous. But Mariko saw it as an opening to score an advantage, and she used her sweet and girlish smile on him to bring it home. Parker may not be a lecher but he is a man. My guess is that when it comes to Mariko, our tough old detective isn't very tough anymore.

The attention was still on Mariko. To get us back on a business track she asked, "Boss, is there any reason to believe the package contained anything other than cash?"

"No—but how much?"

Mariko continued, "What difference would the amount make?"

"That might tell us something. If nothing else, knowing the amount might lead us to the mole in the law firm who sold the casebook to Hudson."

"But, don't we know it was Maxwell?" Mariko had a puzzled look on her face.

"I don't think so, or at least I have my doubts—which brings up more questions."

Sam Littleton cut in. "As far as the amount is concerned, I should be able to help you. The Treasury requires banks to report cash transactions of $10,000 or more. But bank records track all of the cash transactions, even those below the $10,000 level. Most banks have a cooperative relationship with Homeland Security. With respect to commercial accounts, banks will usually give us that information voluntarily when we have what appears to them to be a legitimate need to know. Cash transactions below the $10,000 limit on commercial accounts don't involve the name of individuals so the banks are not sticklers for court authority. Give me the dates you are interested in and let me see what I can find out."

Bryan gave Sam the date the package was picked up by UPS for overnight delivery. Sam then used his laptop to pass the information and his instructions to the regional FBI office and his group attached to the Homeland Security task force he chaired.

I continued, "I'm not convinced that Maxwell was the mole. Nelson at Hudson Mortgage agreed to give me the name of their source once the settlement paperwork with the Fenios is completed. But from my conversation with him, I don't believe there was ever a face-to-face between their mole and the people at Hudson."

Detective McGovern said, "The law firm's security system records the ID number of personnel entering the building after hours. According to the log, Maxwell entered the building minutes after Lansden's death. We questioned him about it; he claimed it wasn't him. He maintains that he lost his original ID badge and got a replacement months ago."

I replied, "What if he is telling the truth? What if someone is impersonating Maxwell? We could be dealing with identity theft."

Tony looked at Detective McGovern and asked impatiently, "Can't you just haul Maxwell's ass into the police interrogation room and grill him until you find out what he knows and doesn't know? Is he involved in the murders? Is he the mole or not?"

The detective answered, "It isn't that simple. After I questioned him about the ID card, he clammed up—would do little more than give us the equivalent of name, rank, and serial number. He is a lawyer and wouldn't answer any more of my questions. I don't think he was hiding anything as much he was showing us that cops and lawyers are like oil and water. I can't get more out of him without declaring him a suspect—and at that point, you can bet that he would lawyer up, as they say."

Bryan spoke up, "Isn't Maxwell just a distraction from the real issue of who murdered Lansden?"

"You could be right, Bryan," I said. "That would be the case if our mole were really Maxwell. If he is, then the whole Hudson thing is just an aside. There is a crime involved, but it isn't the one we are trying to solve. On the other hand, if someone is impersonating Bill Maxwell or using him, then it may matter very much."

Tony asked, "How so?"

"It leads us back to the notion of a criminal mind. Temptation and desperation can lead one astray, but when you encounter someone who will commit multiple crimes then there is seldom a line, such as murder, that he or she will not cross. If we have someone calculating enough to steal information from the firm, blackmail a client, and lift the identity of another person, then they have an evil, criminal mind. We need to know if that is what we are dealing with. My gut still tells me that Maxwell is a patsy, a fall guy. Someone else is masterminding this. No, that's not it; it's different. He is *manipulating* people—controlling them. What I see is a puppeteer—someone pulling the strings." I paused for a second and then asked, "Bryan, one of your guys has already met with the manager of that Spring Hill UPS Store, right?"

"Yes... Tim Rudolph. He lives in Spring Hill."

"Good. Have your guy download photos of the legal staff off the law firm's Web site. Omit their names. Set up a secure spot on our own Web site. Get the manager to look at the photos and pick out Bill Maxwell or anyone he recognizes."

"What if he doesn't remember?"

"He might not, but it's worth a shot. We have nothing to lose."

"Okay, Chief." Bryan used his case room workstation to pass instructions to Tim.

Getting back to the unanswered questions, I said, "Another one of the questions that had been troubling me involved the UPS mailbox. Why did H.T. feel the need to rent the mailbox in Spring Hill not long before his death? Just before this meeting, I got the answer. Apparently H.T. had caught his wife having an affair. Probably in preparation for a divorce proceeding, he was removing some activities and correspondence from her eyes, thus the mailbox. I wouldn't be surprised to find that he had hired a private investigator. Parker, you probably know your way around the Nashville P.I. community. Can you ask around?"

"Already have, and you're right. Actually, I didn't have to go looking; Ed Milbank called me right after the H.T. shooting hit the news. Milbank had taken some pictures of Mrs. Lansden and an unidentified male—tall, athletic build. According to the motel registration form, it was a Phillip Townhouse, but that's probably an alias. After Milbank showed the pictures to H.T., Lansden called him off the case. Apparently, he recognized the man and didn't need Ed to pursue the matter any further."

"What about the pictures, Parker?"

"Milbank gave the photos and the memory card to Lansden. The P.I. didn't keep any copies. He explained that giving up the pictures and digital images keeps him, the P.I., from being forced to turn them over in response to a subpoena."

"Great info, Parker. That leaves us with the question: where are the photos now?"

Bryan asked, "That is where the lockbox comes in, right?"

I nodded and said, "Right! We know that H.T. rented a lockbox in a Spring Hill bank at the same time he leased the UPS mailbox. That is where those photos must be. They can tell us with whom Amber was having an affair. If Amber was the drunken shooter, the odds are her lover is the person who shot and killed H.T. What about it, Parker? Can you get us into that lockbox?"

While the detective was mulling over the possible approaches for getting access to the lockbox, someone timidly opened the case room door and interrupted, "Mr. Rollins, can I see you outside for just a moment?"

CHAPTER 32

Contract Kill

It was Rob Randall, one of our instructors, who interrupted our meeting to speak with me. Rob Randall is an alias. Rob was born Roberto Greco Jr., the son of a New Jersey mafia don. With his father's blessings, Rob had broken away from the life of his father and the long line of Grecos before him. Rob and his wife were under witness protection services. Like a number of the instructors and personal trainers at the WH Club, he hoped to become successful in the music business. He is a talented behind-the-scenes songwriter. I had gotten Rob and his wife out of a bit of trouble a number of months back.

Roberto Greco Sr. considered that a personal favor for which he bore an obligation to repay. Since then, I have been under the protective eye of the don. The details of that saga are chronicled in the book *Mark Rollins' New*

Career and the Women's Health Club. The don keeps track of my activities, especially my travel plans. When I travel to New York, there is always a car and driver waiting for me compliments of the Greco family.

There is a saying in the mafia community about people under their protection but not a member of the family—*he is a friend of mine.* In my case, my friend is *the boss,* the don, and that is a thousand notches higher up than just being a friend of a friend. No one in the worldwide community of organized thieves may touch me without the blessings of Signore Greco.

"What's so urgent, Rob?"

"My father called and asked me to speak with you."

"About what?"

"Someone was shopping a contract on you. As a matter of courtesy, they consulted my father, of course, since you are a known friend of the family," Rob whispered.

"Did your father say who wanted the contract?"

"He didn't know. The consultation was at his level, don to don, and not from the torpedo who dealt with the buyer."

"Torpedo? I seem to remember that's the term the Russian mafia uses for their contract assassins. So whoever the shopper was, he was dealing with the Russians?"

"Pop used the word 'torpedo' so I would think so."

"And is the contract in place?"

"No, Pop nixed it; but he wanted you to understand that does not mean you and your team are out of danger. The shopper could have gone elsewhere—to some local willing to kill you for a few thousand dollars. Or, as my father said, he may be the type who is willing to get his own hands dirty. The point is you need to protect yourself and your family."

"I understand, Rob. Please tell your father that I value his friendship, and I will heed his advice."

"Pop is not expecting me to call him back. It's risky for us to contact each other."

"You're right, of course, Rob. I'm sorry to have caused this risk to you."

"Mr. Rollins, my father also wanted you to know that he would send you some people if you wanted them. He gave me this phone number you can use."

I took the folded paper with the don's phone number as I said, "No, no, I have Tony and Mariko. The three of us can handle this. I will call your father and let him know. I need to thank him personally anyway." I thanked Rob for passing along the information, and he headed back downstairs.

I returned to the case room just as Sam was explaining to the others what he had found out about the contents of the package. "On the day of shipment, the Hudson Bluff Mortgage company purchased at least 30,000 euros. The purchases were spread across several banks obviously to avoid attention. They clearly were trying to stay below the bank reporting requirements. There may have been more, but 30,000 is all we were able to identify."

Detective McGovern said, "What the shit would he want with euros?"

That is when it hit me. "A contract payment!"

McGovern questioned, "A what?"

"A contract killing. It was payment for a contract killer. A professional hit where euros are the currency—France!"

The detective thought for a second and then said, "You're talking about Amber Lansden's murder?"

"You're damn right I am. It ties together."

The detective asked, "Don't you think that's far-fetched? Sounds like a *big* mental jump to me."

I was unwavering. "No, Parker, it isn't as much of a jump as you think. I just found out that someone was shopping a contract *on me*. If they were doing that, I think we can assume that they have done it before. They know the ropes."

Sam shook his head in disbelief as he said, "Mark, you certainly know how to jump in the middle of a snake pit. How you manage to stay alive, I don't know."

"Sam, I'm a *friend of the family.*"

McGovern said, "Holy shit! They said you had friends in high places, but I didn't know that included the *mafia*!"

"Parker, it isn't exactly a friendship I set out to forge, but at times I'm grateful for the connection. I have the good guys like Sam and my friend from New Jersey to thank for my longevity, but let's get back to our task of nailing H.T.'s killer. What about the lockbox, Parker?"

The detective apparently decided to let the mafia connection go for now as he said, "I don't think we have enough for a subpoena yet. We could ask the executor for permission."

"Parker, that's Tillman. We can't rule him out as a suspect. He probably doesn't know about the lockbox. If we tip our hand and he is involved in H.T.'s death, that would be a bad move."

"I assume you mean he might refuse to give us access and then destroy whatever is in the lockbox before we can get at it."

Bryan said, "I have a new micro camera that's designed to insert through a keyhole. If I can get into the vault, I could at least determine the contents of the box. I might actually be able to lift a copy of one of the photos if they're in there."

The idea appeared to make McGovern a little uncomfortable, but he decided to look the other way. The rest of us agreed it was our best shot for now. Bryan would rent a box, and when the bank personnel left him alone with his box, he would use his new toy in an effort to get us the answer we desperately wanted—the answer to the question of what is in the lockbox. Unfortunately that meant we would not have the answer until later— tomorrow at the earliest.

CHAPTER 33

Owen Santo

"Mariko, what about Owen Santo? What are the questions and the answers?"

"Boss, I'm pretty sure Owen Santo is embezzling from the law firm. We know he is living well beyond the level justified by his salary. There are two likely methods—payments to bogus vendors or placing ghost employees on the payroll. But I don't have evidence. I intend to come up with it tonight. I'm going back after everyone has left for the night; I am going to find those bank statements and payroll records, and if I'm right, I'll nail his stealing little butt."

"Mariko, I don't want you going into the firm alone. Tony, you cover her back."

"Will do, Mr. R."

I looked around the room and said, "We need to know if Owen Santo is dirty. But whether he has his hand in the till or not, the bigger question is: does Owen Santo have any involvement in H.T.'s murder? Any ideas?"

McGovern asserted, "Maybe Lansden found out Santo was stealing from him and was going to turn him in. That would give Santo a motive."

"Right, Parker, but we know there were two people involved in the H.T. thing. If that were the motive, who would the second person be?"

Bryan said, "We know Maxwell is a regular visitor to Santo's condo. Maybe Maxwell really is the mole. Maybe Santo and Maxwell are partners."

"That's possible," I said, "assuming Maxwell is our man. That question is still up in the air."

Mariko said, "Don't forget, Boss—Santo and Stewart are also pretty tight. Remember how much time they spent together when Parker was conducting his interviews."

"True, Mariko, and if I remember correctly, you also reported that Santo and Paul Tillman appeared to be having some fairly intense conversations, too. But, here is the deal: if Owen is embezzling, he would have been easy prey for a blackmailer. I just can't see him as the person behind H.T.'s and Amber's deaths. I can't see Santo—a non-lawyer employee of the firm and someone Tillman calls a bookkeeper—as the person H.T. would have had accompanying him out of the building that night. That person was someone H.T. knew very well—someone who had to keep the .25 automatic hidden as they strolled into the Alley together. On the other hand, Santo could be the second person, the drunk, just another puppet whose strings were being pulled by the puppeteer behind all of this."

Detective McGovern said, "If Mariko comes up with proof that Santo is a crook, then I can take him into custody. If he is involved, if someone is using him, we will get it out of him. I think Santo is the kind of person who would give up any co-conspirators in a flash for a deal."

"I agree, Parker." I looked around the table and said, "It's clear we have some more field work to do. We are stumped until we can fill in some more blanks. Agreed?" There were nods all around.

"Mariko, let's either nail Owen Santo or get him off our list of possible bad guys.

Bryan, you have a couple of those blanks to fill in. Have the UPS manager identify the person that picked up the package. Was it Maxwell or was it *someone pretending to be Maxwell*? Second, find out what is inside that mysterious lockbox. We need those answers—ASAP.

Also, Bryan, the next 24 hours are critical. If the killer thinks we are closing in, he could run. Put your team on full watch duty. Monitor any and all cyber activity involving the cast of characters. Let me know on a real-time basis if you encounter any unusual activity.

One last thing Bryan, what about those e-mails Tillman said Amber Lansden sent him?"

"Nothing, Chief. Either he was communicating with her anonymously outside of his office and home systems, or he is damn good at making things disappear."

"That bothers me," I said. "It bothers me a lot."

McGovern asked, "What e-mails?"

"Parker, when no one had heard from Amber, I had suggested that we go to the authorities in an effort to find her. Tillman blew me off by saying that he had received e-mails from her. When I asked for copies, he said he had deleted them. I got the feeling he was lying. The only reason he would have lied is to keep me from looking for her. Maybe he was just protecting her—honoring her wish to be left alone. But as I said, it bothers me. I don't like to be lied to, and I think he did!"

* * *

As Tony and I headed home, I called my son, Dan, and filled him in on my conversation with Rob—letting him know that Rob said someone had tried to hire a hit man to have me killed. Whoever wanted me dead had struck out dealing with the organized crime world thanks to my friends in New Jersey, but there was nothing to stop him from shopping locally for a freelance contractor.

The threat against me doesn't automatically extend to the rest of the family; nevertheless, all of us needed to be vigilant for the next few weeks. Dan and I discussed the need to pay attention to our surroundings and act accordingly. None of us should overreact, but it would be foolish not to be on our toes. Meg had been in the case meeting and was up-to-date on the danger. I had called Sarah before leaving the Club to update her.

We have a safe room in our home, and Sarah decided this was good reason to refresh its supplies—water, power bars, batteries, cell phone chargers, games for the children, etc. Knowing Sarah as I do, I knew that as soon as she could, she would have the grandchildren over to practice. She has an antique whistle, the kind traditionally used by British bobbies. When Sarah blows that whistle, everyone rushes to the safe room—no arguing, no buts, no maybes—just run to the room. That is the rule.

Sarah has her own armory of antique axes, but she also has a small pistol, a Spanish .32 automatic with white plastic grips, which is usually locked away. It is a pocket gun that she can easily carry in her jeans or in her purse when going out. She agreed to do just that—to carry the pistol on her person for the duration.

CHAPTER 34

The Painter

The cornerman saw him walking up and grinned. "So you're back, man. I dig the cover and the shades. Throw in that Titans cap on the deal?"

"No cap, just the $500 as promised. Where is he?"

"Right here, man."

The cornerman pointed to a mature black man sitting on the bus stop bench. He appeared to be relaxing as if waiting for the next bus—arms stretched across the back of the bench, one leg resting across his knee. But this was no pimp or cornerman. He wore alligator tasseled slippers without socks. Light brown trousers. The perfectly laundered white custom dress shirt was open at the neck. The cuffs were French. The links were gold. He wore a ring—diamond but tasteful. His hair was close cut with graying temples. The man smiled, took down one arm, and patted the bench.

As the customer sat down, the man on the bench said, "I understand you have a house that needs painting. I paint houses if the price is right, and the job is manageable." The man was black, but there was no hint of a black accent.

"Paint?"

He chuckled. "You and I know what we mean. The last man that ever saw Jimmy Hoffa was a house painter, too."

"Oh. Okay. I'm offering $15,000 for a paint job."

"Tell me about the man that lives in the house."

"He owns a fitness club, but he is rich. He has a guy who drives him and a woman who works for him that I think is his bodyguard."

"Bodyguard? Sounds like his house is too big for a $15,000 paint job. Give me the name of this man, and I'll give you a quote after I check it out."

"His name is Mark Rollins."

"Where do I find him?"

"He lives in Franklin. His fitness club, the Women's Health Club, is in Brentwood. I have a folder for you with more details: photos, addresses, and phone numbers."

The painter took the folder and asked, "How do I get in touch with you?"

"I would rather contact you."

The painter reached down on his side of the bench and lifted a small satchel. He removed a cell phone from the bag—the kind of phone that has prepaid call time and you can buy it just about anywhere. He gave the phone to his prospective customer. "Let's do it this way. I'll call you at the number of that throwaway phone when my quote is ready. Does that work for you?"

"Okay."

* * *

When it finally came, the customer quickly answered the "painter's" call.

There were no wasted greetings as the painter said, "That is a very tall house. Easy to get hurt on that job. You want a good job, it'll cost you $20,000."

"When can you do the job?"

"Takes time to do it right—maybe two or three weeks."

The customer didn't like that answer. "I'm in a hurry."

"Have to be careful on a house that tall," cautioned the painter.

"I don't like to dawdle—there is a five grand bonus if you get it done this week."

There was a pause. "Okay, my man, you got yourself a contractor, but I need half up front. One thing you need to know is that I insist on prompt payment. I won't look for you unless I have to for my payment. If I look for you, I will find you."

The customer said nothing for several seconds and then said, "How do I get the money to you?"

"I'll be on the bench in 15 minutes. I'll wait for you for 30 minutes, that's all. You deliver it."

"Suppose I send somebody?"

"No, man, this is a private transaction."

"Okay."

The painter disconnected the call.

CHAPTER 35

Peytonsville Road

Tony and I had not yet made it home. The traffic was bad in Brentwood, and we were just passing Murray Lane when a call came through the Lexus' navigation system. It indicated that the caller was unidentified. I answered anyway.

"Mr. Rollins?"

"Yes, this is Mark Rollins."

"I have some information that may be of interest to you."

"Who is this?" It was a male voice—not very distinctive—and I couldn't detect an accent.

"That's not important, but what I have to tell you is."

"What is this information regarding?"

"Not over the phone. If you want what I have, it will cost you five Benjamins. Take I-65 South. Get off at the Goose Creek Exit and go east on Peytonsville Road. Just as you cross the interstate, you will find an abandoned building on your left. Pull in the parking area. Keep your cell phone handy. I won't wait more than 30 minutes so do it now!"

The caller disconnected. I leaned forward from the backseat and asked Tony, "Did you hear that?"

"Yeah, Mr. R. We're coming up on Concord Road. You want me to hang a left and get on I-65?"

"Let's do it, Tony. I'm assuming that the caller has some information about H.T.'s death, and we're only 10 minutes away from Goose Creek—I think that's Exit 61."

The drive was a quick one from Concord Road. Tony pulled into the parking area making a u-turn to position the car for a fast getaway.

I looked around. My gut started talking to me fast. After warning my family about the hit man danger, I had failed to take my own advice. "Tony, this doesn't feel right to me. Keep the motor running and be ready..." My instructions were interrupted by the incoming call. I answered, "This is Mark Rollins."

"Get out of the car. I want to see you."

"Not on your life. I'll give you five minutes. If you are not here, in this parking area, standing next to my car, I'm out of here. So, what about it?"

I got my answer. It came as hot lead from the muzzle of an automatic weapon! Our caller rose from the high grass on our left and began spraying the car. I recognized the distinctive profile of a Tavor TAR-21 rifle. The new smaller caliber NATO rounds used by the TAR-21 were not enough to penetrate the armored sides of the Lexus— but they sure as hell were going to do a job on Black Beauty's glossy exterior. The TAR-21 can fire at the rate of 750 rounds per minute, but the magazine holds only 30 rounds, and it takes 2.4 seconds to empty that clip. Before the shooter could empty it, Tony had hit the accelerator, and we raced out of range.

Apparently, the puppeteer had found his local hit man, one intent on taking me out! The question now is: when and where would he try again? Right now the adrenaline was pumping and the flight instinct took over. I watched our back, and Tony drove with determination. Relying on instinct and experience, Tony headed north on I-65 and then west on I-24. We drove until we were sure that no one was following us. Then we turned back toward home base. We had used up the rush of adrenaline Mother Nature supplies when you are faced with danger. Now the flight response was replaced with good old-fashioned *"don't tread on me"* stand-and-fight stubbornness.

But first things first. Now that we could think about something other than our own skins, I called Sarah. I told her that Tony and I had gotten sidetracked, that we would be home within the hour, and that I would explain later. Then I called Littleton.

"Sam, this is Mark Rollins."

"What's up?"

"Someone just tried to drill me with a Tavor TAR-21!"

"Good Lord!" Littleton bellowed.

"Sam, this happened right off of Exit 61 on Interstate 65 less than an hour ago. That stretch between Franklin and State Route 840 has a serious traffic problem during rush hours, so maybe the Tennessee Department of Transportation has cameras all along that stretch. Do you think you could access those digital files? Their cameras may have recorded the shooter arriving before we did or leaving the area right after my Lexus."

"Mark, you are just a goddamn trouble magnet! Okay, I'll go to work on the TDOT angle and see what we can find. Given the weapon involved, the shooter was a professional. The TAR-21 is new on the scene. The name is an acronym for *Tavor Assault Rifle for the 21st Century.* It has become the weapon of choice in movies and TV episodes. It's not cheap though, so your shooter is a serious businessman. He could be new in the area, but if he's a regular, we probably have a file on him. We know who these guys are—there's only a handful of them operating in the Nashville area."

"Sam, where does one go in Nashville to hire someone like that?"

"The same place you go to buy drugs or women."

"I think I'll do some shopping."

"Mark, that is *not* the brightest idea you've ever had! Let me work on this from the FBI's end. I wouldn't be surprised if I have your man in our custody before morning. If he knows who his employer is, he will give him up in a heartbeat. But I should warn you, the chances are that he has no idea who is paying him. These things are usually handled with cash and without names and addresses."

"Okay, Sam, we'll do it your way, at least for now."

* * *

We had just passed the Brentwood Exit when Sam returned my earlier call.

"Well, we found your shooter."

"Fast work! Were you able to find out who hired him?"

"No, but you don't have to worry about him anymore. He never left the scene. Someone put him out of business— for good."

"You mean he's dead?"

"The man is completely and seriously dead!"

"How?"

"Looks like someone ran over him first—rib cage crushed and both legs appear to be broken. Apparently the guy wasn't dead enough for whoever ran over him so they emptied the shooter's own gun into his gut. It was pretty messy."

"Any ideas?"

"Yes, I'm pretty sure; they even left a note behind for you—pinned to what was left of the man's shirt."

"Oh?"

"It read 'Compliments of your Friends.' Mark, we have access to TDOT's system because of our Homeland Security role so we were able to view activity at Exit 61

around the time of your trouble. A few minutes after you
came screaming back onto the interstate, a black Cadillac
Escalade with New Jersey plates also left the scene. They
are probably out of state by now. What I think, Mark,
is that your friends up north in New Jersey have been
covering your back."

"Sam, they offered, and I told them, **no way**!"

"I believe you, Mark. Unfortunately when they rubbed
out the shooter, they also eliminated any opportunity to
find out who hired him."

"What about the shooter's car? Can you learn anything
from it?"

"We found the car close by, but it was a dead end for
us. The vehicle had been stolen earlier in the day from
one of those self-serve parking lots. Your shooter clearly
knew what he was doing. He took the time to disable
security cameras for the parking facility. If he hadn't, we
would have gotten his picture hot-wiring the car. He also
did a professional job wiping the vehicle clean of finger
prints."

"All that figures. Are you looking for the Escalade?"

"It's no use. We ran the Escalade plates and they are
counterfeit. By now I'm sure they have ditched the vehicle
and switched to something else. But I suggest you let your
'friends' know that when you say 'no thanks,' you mean
it. We don't take kindly to having their kind of help. We
might not be able to pin this on them, but we know who
they are, and they don't want the FBI looking at them too
hard. Let them know that is a personal message from me

to them. Between you and me, the truth is they just made the world a better place, but that is our job, not theirs."

* * *

"Tony, get me home. It is time for a martini—more than one I think."

"Roger, Mr. R. Unfortunately, my day isn't over. I still have to pick up Mariko at her condo. Remember, Boss, I'm playing nursemaid while she does her cat burglar thing tonight. It's going to be a long evening—but, you know, Boss, getting shot at is better than NoDoze! I don't think I could sleep anyway."

"We all have our burdens, my man. I have to explain to Sarah what took us so long to make a normal 20-minute drive from the Club to the house."

CHAPTER 36

Mariko's Caper

Unfortunately, the martini had to wait. I had just finished explaining the evening's events to Sarah and was attempting to defend, without success, my stupidity for agreeing to meet the caller in the first place when Bryan called.

"Chief, we got to the UPS manager before the store closed. After he looked at the photos of the law firm's attorneys, he was absolutely clear about one thing."

"What's that?"

"Whoever picked up the package, it was not Bill Maxwell. Unfortunately, the manager was not as sure about who the person using Maxwell's ID was. He picked out the new partner, Herb Stewart, as a possibility, but he wouldn't swear to it."

"Why is he so sure it was not Maxwell?"

"He said he played basketball in college and belongs to an amateur adult team that plays once a month. Maxwell is just average in the height department. The person who picked up the package was tall. The UPS manager remembers thinking to himself that he wished the guy was on their basketball team."

"Bryan, that description could fit Tillman, too."

"Yes, but the UPS guy says he thinks the impersonator was younger than Tillman. He didn't rule Tillman out as a possibility. He just thought Stewart was the best match. Still, as I said, the man wasn't sure enough for a positive ID. He said he would not testify to it."

"Bryan, this makes that lockbox more important than ever. If it turns out that Stewart was also the man having an affair with Amber Lansden, then I think we would have to conclude that Herbie is our man."

"I'll get the pictures, Chief, one way or another. There is one more thing... Tillman just purchased a handgun."

"How do you know?"

"If you purchase a gun in Tennessee, there is a required background check. It was done via the Internet and that is where we picked it up. As you requested, we are spidering the Internet for anything related to players involved in this thing. When our spiders find something, it is added to our search catalog on the H.T. case database server."

"What did he purchase?"

"A Kimber® .45 caliber handgun. It's their Ultra Crimson Carry II model—a single-action compact autoloader with a built-in laser sight."

"Does he have a concealed carry license?"

"No, but that never stops the bad guys from buying a gun."

"Come on, Bryan, we don't know that Tillman is up to anything other than self-protection. Remember, the police took his revolver. Let me ask you a question. If you were a partner in a law firm where your partner and his wife were just murdered, what would you do?"

"I would buy a gun."

"Exactly! I don't think we can assume there is anything sinister here, but since it is a concealed carry weapon, I think we need to communicate this to members of our case team. You are the control point. Send them the info."

"Will do, Chief."

"What about the Stewart thing? Should I pass that info along to everyone in the case room group?"

"Since the UPS folks were not positive on their ID, let's hold off on that until we get back together. Maybe by then we will have something on the contents of the lockbox."

"Right, Chief."

After Bryan and I wrapped up our phone call, I finally got that martini. Sarah made it for me while I was finishing my call. She also poured something for herself—dry vermouth on the rocks, Martini and Rossi, of course. We agreed to forget my rather reckless afternoon adventure. We had dinner, relaxed, and reviewed the defensive precautions to protect our home and extended family.

I decided not to add bodyguards at this time. With the assassin dead, I doubted that our puppeteer would try again—at least for a while. Sam Littleton had promised me that he would work the FBI's sources for a heads-up if someone began shopping for another try at me. I would move quickly to add bodyguards should we have any indication that our mastermind was in the market again.

* * *

It was 1:15 a.m. Mariko used her key card to enter the law office building. Tony remained outside in Black Beauty. The two were in constant contact by way of the Nikto communication devices Bryan had provided to the case room team.

Detective McGovern was also nearby in his official car. He had been too old school to wear the communicator, but from where he was parked, he had a visual on Tony and the Lexus. He was there just in case some of Metro's finest took exception to Tony's presence. Frequent all-nighters by young associates or paralegals working on an important case had desensitized the cops on the beat to late-night lights in the law office. A parked car with a waiting driver was another matter altogether, however. McGovern was prepared to run interference if it became necessary.

It took Mariko less than 30 minutes to find what she was looking for in the bank records. "Got them, Tony. I'm going to start comparing the check register to the cleared checks returned by the bank. If he wrote checks to himself or a dummy company and then later changed the computer records, I should spot the mismatch easily."

Minutes went by, and Tony said, "Mariko, find anything yet? Sooner or later someone is going to want to know what I'm doing out here."

"Tony, no mismatches but three missing checks in the first month I've audited. Santo must have pulled the checks and destroyed them in an effort to cover his tracks. I have written down the check numbers. The bank will have digital images of the checks in their archives. I'll get Bryan working on that in morning. I'm going to check the payroll records next."

"Okay, but make it snappy and keep talking to me," Tony said nervously.

The payroll registers were easy to find. "Tony, I have the payroll registers and a copy of the law firm's current internal phone list. That is the best tool I have for looking for ghost employees. So the question is: will I find one or more payroll checks for names not on the phone list?" Several minutes passed before Mariko shouted, "Bingo!"

Tony asked, "I take it you found your ghost?"

"Right on, Tony, my boy! One Rachel Pappas, an administrative assistant, making $9800 a month. Guess where the accounting codes place her?"

"Mariko, I'm a driver not an accountant; how the hell would I know?"

"Rachel Pappas is being expensed to Herb Stewart's overhead account. Tony, overhead is one of the factors used in determining an attorney's compensation—the higher your overhead, the lower your compensation. Stewart would have to have known she was being charged to his overhead account."

Tony said, "So that means Herb Stewart and Owen Santo are partners in crime."

"What I'm sure of, Tony, is that they both know that Rachel is a ghost employee. As to whom is receiving the benefit of the $9800-a-month salary, I don't know. Herb Stewart is a partner. Santo is just an employee. I suppose Owen could just be doing what Herb Stewart told him to do. You know, like the boss said—puppet and puppeteer."

Tony said, "Damn it, Mariko, I'm getting tired of the questions. Every time we go after an answer, we seem to come away with more questions. I vote for McGovern to sweat Owen; play him against Herb Stewart."

* * *

McGovern's car came to a screeching halt next to Tony's car. He lowered the window of his Ford Crown Victoria and shouted, "Tony, get Mariko out of there! I just got a 10-56 at Herb Stewart's address."

Tony muted his communicator and asked, "What's a 10-56?"

"A suicide." With that, McGovern sped off to the Stewart residence.

Tony took his Nikto off mute. "Mariko, shut it down!"

"What's up, Tony?"

"Parker was just here. There has been a suicide—sounds like Herb Stewart."

"I'm on my way."

CHAPTER 37

10-56

Tony's call woke me up at 2:30 a.m. The Stewarts live on Tyne near its intersection with Belle Meade Boulevard. McGovern had gone straight there. Tony and Mariko decided to pick me up first since I don't live far from there, and then the three of us would go to Herb Stewart's home.

When we got there, the coroner had already bagged the body for transport. McGovern immediately began filling us in on the details. "Single shot through the roof of his mouth and into the brain. The weapon in his hand was the Beretta Modelo 418 registered to Amber Lansden. He left a suicide note. Typed, or I should say prepared on his computer, and printed. It is still up on his display… printed copy beside the body… no signature… confesses to shooting H.T. Lansden with the same pistol. The note also identifies Mrs. Lansden as an accomplice—the diversion shooter. He goes into detail about how she used Tillman's revolver and put on the act of being drunk. Frankly, it's more like a suicide short story than a damn note. It's a hell of a lot longer than any suicide note I've ever seen. Anyway, according to what Stewart wrote, he and Amber Lansden were lovers. H.T. found out about it and was going to divorce her and force Stewart out of the firm. They stood to lose everything."

"What about Amber Lansden's murder?" I asked.

"He didn't take any blame for her death. In fact he cited her death as the last straw—typical crap about having nothing left to live for."

"That's strange.

"How so?"

"Parker, I'm pretty damn sure that Amber's murder was a contract killing. Stewart confessed to everything else, why wouldn't he come clean about Amber?"

"Mark, maybe you're wrong. Maybe her death is unrelated."

"Right... and maybe pigs really can fly! No, Parker, Amber was killed because our killer couldn't trust her to hold up under questioning from authorities. I suppose she was coming unglued. Who knows... maybe she was also making unwanted demands on her married lover... pressing him to end his marriage."

"So you don't think the Stewart confession closes this case?" The detective's question reflected his disappointment.

"I have my doubts. Where is Stewart's wife?"

"According to neighbors she is visiting relatives in Connecticut. We are trying to contact her now."

"So Stewart was home alone?"

"Yes."

"Parker, did you search the body?"

"Yes."

"Find anything of interest?"

"Yes, I found Bill Maxwell's missing ID and key card."

"That fits. Bryan got a tentative identification of the person who picked up the package of euros. According to the UPS manager, it was Stewart using Maxwell's ID."

The coroner walked up to us and said to McGovern, "Detective, I'm done here. I'll give you a full report when we have completed the autopsy."

I asked the coroner, "Did you see anything that would make you question the suicide scenario?"

"There are a couple of chipped teeth. That could have happened from the gun's recoil, or it could be due to someone forcing the gun into his mouth."

"A .25 caliber gun doesn't have much recoil," Mariko pointed out.

The coroner replied, "Yes, but it might have been enough. When we do our complete examination at the autopsy, we will look for pressure bruises on the neck and back of the head. If someone forced the gun into the victim's mouth, we should see some evidence of it."

Detective McGovern said, "Doc, we need to know the minute you see anything that contradicts a suicide. Can you put his autopsy at the top of your list?"

"It will be number one on our schedule tomorrow." The coroner nodded to our small group and turned to leave.

"Mark, I have to say that as far as Metro is concerned, Stewart's note means this case is closed unless the doc gives us reason to doubt the suicide."

"I understand."

* * *

As Tony drove Mariko and me back to my house, we talked about Tillman's gun purchase. In light of the warning from Rob's father, I was carrying my Sig P232 in an ankle holster. I suggested that Tony and Mariko take similar steps until we were sure that any danger had been eliminated. The attempted contract on my life was one reason I had trouble buying the Stewart suicide. You don't try to arrange for someone to be killed and then go kill yourself.

Tony said, "Well, if it wasn't a suicide, why do you think Herbie-boy had his ticket punched?"

"Let's say Stewart was in on H.T.'s death as was Amber Lansden. Now both are dead. Doesn't that sound to you like someone covering his tracks—eliminating anyone who could finger him?"

"So Stewart was in on H.T.'s death, too."

"Absolutely. I don't think there is any question about that, but that is not necessarily the end of the story. I suspect Herbie, as you like to call him, got what he deserved, but there was someone else pulling the strings. Our puppeteer is still out there."

Tony said, "Well, Mr. R., you don't have a lot of possibilities left. Doesn't it come down to either Tillman or the administrator guy, Santo?"

Mariko said, "Boss, Santo was embezzling from the firm by writing checks to himself. I'm convinced of it, and before the day is over, I will have copies of the checks to prove it. I also found a ghost employee that has been charged against Stewart's account at the firm. That means Stewart knew about it."

"So maybe Santo and Stewart were working together. Mariko, do you really think Santo is dominant enough to have Stewart as his lapdog?"

"I think I see where you are going, Boss. If they were working together, Stewart would have been the puppeteer pulling the strings. But his puppet, Santo, could have decided to cut the strings by killing his master—Stewart."

"Yes, Mariko, it could be that way. We need to look a little closer at Owen Santo. What was the name of the ghost employee?"

Mariko answered, "Rachel Pappas."

When Mariko told me her name, it put a different light on things. "Mariko, she is a *real person*, a stripper, and I bet you she was Herb Stewart's mistress. Stewart probably found out Santo was dipping into the till and blackmailed him into putting Stewart's squeeze on the payroll. Based on what I know about Herbie, Rachel Pappas is more his type than Amber Lansden. I don't think Herbie was Amber's lover, but I'll lay you ten to one that our puppeteer was. At least Amber was having an affair with him. As for love, I doubt seriously that our puppeteer ever loved her or anyone else."

It was 5:00 a.m. when we pulled into my drive.

"Let's have some coffee and breakfast. We have some planning to do. It's time to bring this thing to a head. As it stands, it looks like we could always be waiting for another piece of this puzzle to fall in place. It may be time to add a little bluff to what we already have and confront our puppeteer."

CHAPTER 38

The Money

By 6:30 a.m., Tony had returned Mariko to her condo and then retreated to his apartment. Sarah had joined me on our screened-in porch for a cup of coffee.

Bryan's phone call interrupted us.

"What is it, Bryan?"

"Chief, the money is gone."

"What do you mean?"

"The insurance money... the $17 million. It was transferred early this morning to a Wells Fargo account in California, and from there it was split into two equal wires, one to Andorra, and the second to Monaco. From there we believe the funds were moved to a bank in Liechtenstein, and as far as we can tell, that's the end of the trail—but it might as well be on the moon because it is now beyond the reach of anyone except the person who moved it."

"And who would that be? Let me guess—Mr. Paul Tillman, Esquire."

"Sorry, Chief. The person who moved it was also traveling last night. Owen Santo flew to Atlanta at 7:22 p.m. on Delta. It was a round-trip ticket returning a week from today, but we have no evidence that he is checked into any area hotel. Nor has he rented a car or used his credit cards since landing in Atlanta."

"What do you think happened to Mr. Santo?"

"Chief, I suspect that he flew from Atlanta to Miami or maybe to New York under an assumed name. Then, I think he would have departed the states on an international flight, probably under another assumed name and false passport. The multiple ID changes are standard operating procedure if you want to cover your tracks, and he did. My guess is that Mr. Owen Santo has disappeared with $17,000,000! And, I bet he will be a hard man to find. You want me to take on that task?"

"No, Bryan. Our administrator is an embezzler and a thief, but there's someone who deserves that $17,000,000 even less. Whether it was his intent or not, Owen Santo just doled out a little justice of his own, and I'm glad of it. Sooner or later Owen Santo will meet his fate without our help—*ut sementem feceris ita metes*—as you sow so will you reap."

Sarah had listened to my conversation with Bryan. H.T. had not only been a great man, he had been a friend.

She put her hand on my arm and asked the simplest of questions, "What now, Mark?"

"Right now the police think Herbert Stewart killed himself. If that sticks then they will also accept the confession and close the case. I don't believe it. I don't believe his suicide note. I sure as hell don't think Herbert Stewart and his supposed lover, Amber, acted on their own to kill H.T. Whatever their exact role was, they were being used.

I've thought for some time that there was someone pulling the strings—someone arrogantly hiding behind lesser people whose hands did his dirty work. Stewart and Amber were greedy and needy people, easily manipulated because of their weaknesses. They were nothing but puppets whose strings were being pulled by their master who, for his own preservation and lust for money, has now killed three people—H.T., Amber, and Stewart.

Sarah, it is time for this to end. I'm not waiting for any more questions or answers. I'm going to confront this killer today. I'm afraid if I don't, the man responsible for H.T.'s death will get away with his murder."

"Be careful, Mark; don't become victim number four. There are people who need you, and I'm one of them.

* * *

Mariko had placed micro cameras in several locations in the law firm the night before at my suggestion. One of those was in Paul Tillman's office. I selected the secure portion of the WH Club's Web site that displayed the camera feeds. Paul Tillman was at his desk, blissfully unaware that $17,000,000 had disappeared from the firm's investment accounts the night before. How would he react when he learned the news?

I called Mariko and told her to stay away from the law office until I advised her otherwise. Then I headed for the shower and a short power nap.

CHAPTER 39

The Puppeteer

A trip to the law office meant suit and tie rather than my customary black polo shirt and khaki pants. That was okay with me because I didn't want to make this trip to Lansden, Tillman and Hall without firepower. Thus for my shirt, I opted for a blue button-down oxford designed for covert work. The center button is a fake. The actual closure device is a quick-release snap. Under the oxford is a spandex holster undershirt from 5.11's Tactical Series with an integrated underarm shoulder holster. The outfit is designed for full concealment with rapid-draw access to the holstered handgun—in this case my Sig.

* * *

Tony was driving Black Beauty and, as usual, was dressed for the part: black suit, white shirt, thin black tie, and chauffeur's hat. Tony's jacket concealed his weapon of choice, an expandable tactical baton from ASP, Inc.

I called Mariko from the car. "We'll pick you up at your condo. And, Mariko, if I'm right, we are dealing with someone who kills easily so you need to be armed—but keep your handgun under wraps. As far as everyone in the firm is concerned, you are still an employee in the accounting department. As for being late, you had a doctor's appointment, and you told Santo yesterday that you would be in a little late today. Santo isn't going to be there to dispute you. Right now people in the firm are probably just beginning to wonder where Santo is."

"So Tillman is our man, right?"

"It looks that way, Mariko. I feel a little like we are performing in an episode of the British TV program, the *Midsomer Murders*, where the killer is the only person in the village left standing."

"Couldn't it still be Owen Santo?"

"It just doesn't fit. Our murderer is a puppeteer who uses people. He had more than just influence. He was able to control them—to bring out the worst in them. Santo is a thief, but he doesn't fit this profile. It was Tillman, not H.T., as Tillman tried to get us to believe, who saw to it that Herb Stewart became a partner. He knew about Stewart's gambling addiction. He knew Stewart owed money to some really bad characters. Tillman probably knew about the stripper mistress. Stewart knew Tillman could pull the floor out from under him anytime he chose to do so.

And, let's face it, Stewart's lust for money was strong enough that Tillman was able to get him to pull the trigger—to kill for a share of the insurance money. Amber was a needy woman—afraid of losing her womanly allure and entering middle age. She fell for Tillman's charm and was seduced by his athletic body. He is, after all, a handsome man. But once H.T. found out about the affair, Amber was at risk of a divorce that would have left her penniless by her upscale standards.

You can be sure that Tillman knew that his days as a partner in the firm controlled by Lansden were going to come to an end. He would be named as a corespondent in the divorce proceedings so that meant that his own marriage would also be headed for the divorce court. His wife would take him to the cleaners for his infidelity. With H.T. out of the way, Tillman would be the head of the law firm. Once the idea of killing H.T. was considered, the large insurance policy must have taken on an irresistible magnetism. Twenty million dollars is a lot of money.

No, it was not Owen. Herb Stewart was the triggerman. Amber was our drunken shooter. Tillman was the puppeteer—he just pulled the strings. Then to protect himself, Tillman killed his accomplices. He killed Amber using a contract assassin. And then with his own hands, he crammed that pistol in Stewart's mouth and blew his brains out."

Tony pulled under the *porte cochere* at the Werthan Mills building. Mariko was waiting for us. She and I ended our phone conversation, and she joined me in the back of the Lexus.

As Mariko got in the car, she asked, "But can you prove it, Boss? We still don't have any hard evidence to prove that Tillman masterminded H.T.'s murder or killed the others."

"No, Mariko, but I hope to get that proof today."

"Just how are you going to do that, Boss?"

"By talking shop with him. You know the old saying *'It takes a thief to catch a thief.'* I plan to convince Tillman that I am just as much of a criminal as he is."

As Tony pulled into the parking garage used by the law firm, Mariko asked, "You really expect him to admit that he masterminded Lansden's death?"

"I do—one lowlife to another."

"This should be interesting."

Just before we left the car for the short walk to the law office, I called Bryan. "Bryan, I want you to get in touch with Detective McGovern. Tell him I have decided to confront Tillman in his office to get a confession out of him. I'm going to wear the communicator. Record what is said and patch Parker in so he can listen. Make sure he wears the damn earpiece."

"Chief, McGovern isn't going to like this."

"I didn't ask his permission."

"Chief, isn't this just a little dangerous?"

"I have Tony and Mariko with me. I think we can handle him."

"What if you can't?"

"Bryan, thanks for your concern, but we are doing this. Just get Parker plugged in for me."

"Will do, Chief, but *be careful.*"

* * *

Tillman's secretary, teary-eyed over the report of Stewart's suicide, ushered the three of us into Tillman's office. Without looking up from the document he was reading, Tillman asked, "What is it now, Mark? Can it wait? I'm up to my neck dealing with this new tragedy." When I didn't answer immediately, he looked up and saw Mariko and Tony with me. There was a curious expression on his face as he asked, "What is this? Mariko, what are you doing here? Why aren't you in accounting?"

Without being asked, Mariko and I sat down in the side chairs in front of Tillman's desk. Mariko said nothing, but I did. "Paul, you know that I ran a high-tech company."

"Yes, what about it?"

"I still have high-powered technology people working for me. My team can do almost anything over the Internet—and that includes getting into your system and the systems of your banks and investment firms."

"What does that have to do with me?"

"For starters, it means I know you purchased the contract on Amber's life. You killed Herb Stewart and tried to make it look like a suicide to cover up your role in H.T.'s death. And here is the real kicker... as of this moment, you have done it all for naught!"

"What the hell are you talking about?"

"Did you know that H.T. hired a private detective who took pictures of you and Amber?"

Tillman said nothing.

"Yes, he did." I had decided to bluff. "H.T. kept them in a lockbox. Now I have those pictures."

"Bullshit. You're lying. You forget I'm the executor of H.T.'s estate. I've been through all of his lockboxes."

"No, Paul, you haven't. You apparently didn't know about this one. You knew about his secret UPS mailbox, the one you used as the ship-to address for the euros you got from Hudson Bluff. The euros you had Stewart pick up for you. The euros you used to purchase the contract on Amber. You knew about the mailbox because of the monthly rental checks. What you didn't know is that H.T. also had a secret lockbox in a Spring Hill bank. There were no monthly rental statements; he paid for it a year in advance."

Paul Tillman glared at me with cold black eyes. His jaw locked and hands balled into a fist. The usual smirk was now an unquestionable sneer! He looked at me with the hate of a superior being challenged by some lowlife. All dignity and civility left him.

My first bluff about the pictures had worked so I went for number two. "By the way, Paul, when you purchased your new handgun, the Kimber .45, you were fingerprinted. Your prints were filed by the gun store with the State of Tennessee. You did a pretty good job wiping down Amber's little Beretta, the one you wanted us to believe Stewart used to kill himself. But you were not perfect. The authorities found a partial, and it matched your prints."

Tillman's skill as a defense attorney quickly dismissed the importance of the fingerprint. "My print could have gotten on that gun at any time."

Bluff number two was a dud so I pulled out bluff number three. "Paul, I don't suppose you knew that Amber wrote me a letter? Amber knew that H.T. had called me for help. She thought I was a friend that could help her avoid being put away for the rest of her life. Her letter to me was a cry for help, and in it she tells all. She tells how you masterminded H.T.'s death. How Herb Stewart used her gun to kill H.T. How he muffled the sound by firing the gun from inside one of the law firm's leather portfolios. She tells how she played the role of the drunk and that she used your revolver to distract any would-be witnesses."

I could see Tillman beginning to realize that I knew too much… beginning to realize that I must be after something. Why else would I be telling him what I knew and not the police? Feeling more in charge, his face relaxed, and he asked, "What do you want?"

"Actually, Paul, I don't want anything. I already have it."

He was having trouble understanding. His eyebrows rose. His forehead tightened as he exhaled the word, "What?"

"Your $17,000,000—that's what I meant when I said that as of this very moment you have done it all for nothing."

Paul Tillman's expression was that of a man desperately trying to grasp the meaning of my spoken words. The mental gears were churning. He stood, picked up the phone and buzzed his secretary. "Call Greenwood at the bank." He hung up. His eyes remained fixed on me— hard, cold and unblinking.

The phone rang. He picked it up. "Bob, any unusual activity in my accounts?" I could see his jaw tighten again as he listened. His stare turned from cold to intense hate. Still holding the phone with his left hand, he had reached into the top right drawer of his desk, and the three of us were now staring down the barrel of his 1911 style compact .45.

He said nothing but slowly replaced the receiver back on his phone. When he did speak, he did so very slowly... "I don't know which I want more, to kill you or to get my seventeen million back."

While Mariko and I were seated, Tony had remained standing. Out of the corner of my eye, I had watched Tony remove his baton from his coat pocket as Tillman talked to his banker. Unextended, it is only 9" long. It was now palmed with the still-unexpanded business end going up the back of Tony's coat sleeve. I knew Tony's speed. He could extend the baton and cross the 10 feet between him and Tillman in .5 seconds or less. It was unlikely that Tillman could shift his attention from me to Tony in time to stop a baton attack. Tillman would, however, have plenty of time to shoot me. Tony knew the risk to me so he didn't charge.

Mariko had carried a purse for a change. It had a weapon pocket that opened to the exterior of the bag facing her. The purse was in Mariko's lap shielding the Springfield 9mm EMP that was now in Mariko's hand, locked and loaded. However, Mariko didn't attempt to take out Tillman. Tillman's hand was on the trigger. His weapon was already aimed squarely at me. It would take Mariko less than a quarter of a second to raise her arm and fire her handgun at Tillman's center mass. That would not be fast enough, and Mariko knew it.

My concealed weapon was useless at this point. Unless Tillman was distracted, there was no way I could draw and fire my weapon before Tillman blew a hole through my chest.

But this is what I came for. Now it was time for bluff number four. "You don't want to kill me, Tillman. I'm the only thing that stands between you and the electric chair. Paul, you and I are men of the world. I'm not the police or the judge and jury. Yes, I know you masterminded H.T.'s death, paid to have Amber killed, and even killed Stewart with your own hands; but given the right arrangement between the two of us, I don't have to share what I know with the authorities. The only piece of evidence they have is your fingerprint on the gun. As you said, you can come up with a logical explanation for that print... provided that's all they have. And right now, that *is* all they have to tie you to these murders. I have the rest—the pictures, Amber's letter, the trail that ties you to Amber's death... and, finally, I have the money."

"I don't believe you."

"What don't you believe?"

"Amber would never have written you."

"Why would I lie to you about that? But let's assume for a minute that I *am* lying about the letter. I also have the evidence that you used the euros to buy the murder of Amber."

"How could you possibly know that?"

"Oh, Paul, you are an intelligent man. Think about it. I know you shopped for a contract on me. The first people you dealt with would not accommodate you, right? They turned the business down."

Tillman said nothing so I continued, "Why do you think killers for hire would turn down your good money? Weren't you just a little surprised when they turned you down? Didn't that make you wonder about me? They would not take up your contract on me because I'm a protected person, Paul—a member of the same brotherhood. So you went shopping locally for another alternative. If you don't know already, the man you hired is dead. He was killed by the same brotherhood that turned down your first attempt to hire someone to kill me."

"Rollins, I don't give a crap *who* you are! I'm not going to let you take my money and get away with it. As you said, I worked hard for it."

"Paul, you don't really have a say about that. I already have your money."

"You will never spend it, Rollins, I will *kill* you—*all three of you*. As you seem to know, I have gotten pretty good at this killing thing."

"What good will that do? Paul, I don't have any intention of turning over my evidence to the authorities.

You see, Paul, we are both thieves. I just happen to have had more practice at it. As for the money, I came here today because I want to give some of it back to you."

Tillman's face contorted; his mouth became a sarcastic sneer as he asked, "Out of your good nature, I suppose?"

"Right. You see, Paul, I don't want to worry about you. I don't want to worry that you will keep trying to find someone to put a bullet in me. Or, that you might be brave enough to try to do that on your own. I think I deserve something for the two previous insults—your failed attempts to have me killed. The $5 million you saved by killing Amber will do nicely. The rest of it I'll wire to the account of your choice just as soon as I confirm that you have left the country for good."

"Leave the country? You want me to walk away from everything and everybody I know?"

"Yes, that's the ticket, Paul. I want you gone. That's the price for my returning $12,000,000 to you."

"I can't do that; I might as well be dead."

"What did you think, Paul? Did you really think you could kill three people, pocket all that insurance money, and just continue to enjoy your life as a member of Nashville's elite social class?"

"I didn't set out to kill three people... just H.T. He was going to ruin me. Look, Rollins, you don't have to worry about me. Keep *half* the money but forget about me leaving the country."

I had him. "Keep half... that's funny, Paul."

"Why? You and I both will have eight-and-a-half million—that isn't *funny*! It is *real* money."

"What is funny, Paul, is that you were right to begin with. I have been lying. I don't have your $17 million. I don't have anything to give back to you—or to keep."

His expression was sheer bewilderment as he uttered, "But the bank?"

"Tillman, you were outsmarted but not by me. You were outsmarted by your administrator—the person you keep calling your bookkeeper!"

"Owen?" he asked in disbelief.

"Yes... Owen Santo. He ran off yesterday and took all of the money with him. You have nothing, Paul Tillman—not one red cent. And now you have confessed to three murders—murders that you are going to pay for with you own life. I'm the person that is going to see to it."

Tillman's rage spread across his face. I could taste it in the air. His finger began to tighten on the trigger of the gun still aimed at my midsection. As his grip on the pistol's handle tightened, the gun's laser activated and a red dot appeared in the center of my chest.

I reached for my gun. Tony charged. The baton blow was a glancing one but enough to save my life. I felt the searing heat from Tillman's .45 round as it kissed the skin of my left arm and set off a red shower. The room erupted into a war zone of eardrum-splitting gunshots.

Tillman's one shot was all he had time to make before his body was torn apart by the simultaneous rapid fire from Detective McGovern and Mariko. McGovern was standing in the doorway to Tillman's office having arrived unnoticed just as Tillman admitted to the murders.

Mariko's shots were delivered unsighted from her seated position. McGovern had responded as trained. You never fire your weapon unless there is an immediate danger of death to you or another person. If you do fire your weapon, you don't do it timidly. You don't shoot once and check to see if that disabled the assailant. You fire rapidly and at the largest part of the target. You don't stop firing until your weapon is empty. Tillman was dead before he ever hit the floor. Paul Tillman had drawn first blood. McGovern had responded by emptying his nine-round magazine. Mariko did likewise. The now empty magazine of her EMP had been loaded with six personal defense hollow-point rounds.

The puppeteer was dead—quite dead.

CHAPTER 40

Postmortem

We have a press and liberal elite who paint those who legally own guns for sport or self-defense as hot shots, cowboys, and rednecks. Every shooting becomes an opportunity for the anti-gun lobby to further limit gun owner's rights. Make no mistake; unless there is a radical change in direction, it is only a matter of time before we lose our rights under the Second Amendment. For the anti-gun folks, *the end fully justifies the means.* Rather than amend the Constitution outright, or overturn the traditional interpretation of the Second Amendment, the anti-gun people are coming at us along our flanks. One liberal senator was overheard to say, "The Constitution may provide for the right to own guns, but it doesn't say a damn thing about ammunition!"

Those were the conditions on the field, and the next ten days following the shooting of Paul Tillman, Esq. were a bit of hell. Sam Littleton hadn't been there to lend his good hand to clean things up for me as he had done in previous adventures. Even if he had, I doubt that even he, as head of the regional FBI office, could have controlled the after events this time.

On the official side, Parker McGovern was suspended pending an investigation of the shooting. That has become standard operating procedure for most police departments when an officer uses deadly force. Civilian shooters like Mariko have an even tougher time. Any time a civilian fires a weapon at another person, he is going to spend time in a courtroom. At a minimum, someone is going to sue for wrongful death. Even worse, they face a risk that a prosecutor will decide to file criminal charges against them.

Tillman's wife wasted no time in filing a suit against Mariko. Lawyers always go where the money is. Mariko is my employee so the Women's Health Club and I, Mark Rollins, individually were quickly brought into the suit. The press, of course, had a field day. Tillman had been body drilled, riddled by fifteen rounds of ammunition— nine large caliber shells fired by McGovern and six nine-millimeter shells by Mariko Lee. The coroner's report noted that any one of those fifteen rounds was sufficient to cause death. To the layperson those fifteen pulls of the trigger sound excessive. The press, too lazy to investigate the facts, latched onto the multiple gunshots as evidence of excessive force. No one bothered to point out that both Detective McGovern and Mariko Lee had followed standard procedures in responding to a deadly threat especially where first blood had already been drawn.

Luckily, the press discovered that the whole Lansden sordid affair was an even better story. The insurance motive behind H.T.'s death, Tillman's affair with and then murder of Lansden's wife, the murder of co-conspirator Herbert Stewart, and the missing administrator with seventeen million dollars were a better story than the daytime soaps. The shooting became simply background noise. Mrs. Tillman, jolted by the growing scandal and the paralyzing invasion of TV reporters and satellite trucks, retreated to property she owned in Spain and quietly dropped the suit.

As the press coverage of the shooting was winding down, the four of us, Parker, Mariko, Tony, and me, met for a *postmortem* on the case. The place was Sperry's on Harding Road in Belle Meade. We were still considering the menu when our drinks arrived. Sperry's makes a great Belvedere martini.

Mariko said, "What I don't understand is how so much corruption and criminal behavior can co-exist with goodness. H.T. Lansden certainly would have been governor, and I think he could have risen to President. He was full of good intentions. He wanted to make a better world."

I explained, "Mariko, it is not that unusual for good and evil to coexist in the same space and time. In fact, it is really the norm. It is yin and yang, the other side of the coin. Just look at our political world. Powerful men are elected and sent to Washington to do good. People with less than good intentions flock to that power because the streets around them are paved with gold. I guess I should say the streets are paved with pork or stimulus money. Where there is that much money, there is always corruption. Greed surrounds powerful men like H.T. Unfortunately people like H.T. and others elected for office crave attention. They need to have people around them—people they consider loyal devotees who cheer them on and pump up their egos. That makes people like H.T. easy prey for parasites.

In his case, H.T. never saw the bad side of his followers until it appeared as disloyalty. And it was the worst kind of disloyalty—betrayal by the people closest to him, his wife and his partner. For people like H.T., disloyalty is the ultimate unforgivable sin and cuts the deepest.

Tillman was the antithesis of H.T. He looked down on people. His good manners couldn't hide his contempt. You could see it in his face—the smirk that changed too easily to a sneer when challenged. Tillman looked for and found the weaknesses in others—their greed, their addictions, their perversions, their needs, loneliness, and insecurity. He used those weaknesses like a puppeteer uses strings. He used them to get others to do his bidding, his dirty deeds. He wanted to be King. He wanted it all—H.T.'s wife, the law firm, and the money."

Mariko asked, "What happens to the law firm now?"

"Lansden, Tillman and Hall no longer exists. Hall and some of the associates joined another Nashville law firm.

Most clients who worked with Hall moved to the new firm with him. The others went to the wind. Nothing that H.T. Lansden or Paul Tillman built survived their weaknesses."

"What was Lansden's weakness?"

"The tendency of men like him to confuse loyalty and flattery as a testament to their own greatness. There is an old Norse Proverb that sums it up: *Flattery looks like friendship, just as a wolf looks like a dog.* In the end, it was their vanity that turned their accomplishments into dust. For Lansden, it was his vanity that kept him from seeing beyond the flattery. For Tillman, he thought he could do anything and have everything. To him, people were mere puppets to be manipulated. The thought of failure never occurred to him. He was taking it all, and it would all be his forever. Like amoral tyrants before him, vanity gave him a sense of invincibility or immortality. Shelley captured it in his sonnet, OZYMANDIAS:

I met a traveler from an antique land
Who said: Two vast and trunkless legs of stone
Stand in the desert. Near them on the sand,
Half sunk, a shatter'd visage lies, whose frown
And wrinkled lip and sneer of cold command
Tell that its sculptor well those passions read
Which yet survive, stamp'd on these lifeless things,
The hand that mock'd them and the heart that fed.
And on the pedestal these words appear:
"My name is Ozymandias, king of kings:
Look on my works, ye Mighty, and despair!"

Nothing beside remains. Round the decay
Of that colossal wreck, boundless and bare,
The lone and level sands stretch far away.

Before anyone could comment, my cell phone rang.
"Hello."

"Mr. Rollins, I need to see you," a voice said
anxiously.

"I'm sorry, but I'm dining with friends. May I return
your call later?"

"Please, Mr. Rollins, call me no later than tonight.
I don't care how late! You see, Mr. Rollins, I have a
problem—a big problem—and I need your help!"

Guns and Weapons

Guns and Weapons
in
Mark Rollins and the Puppeteer

Antique Hand Axes: Sarah Rollins has a fondness for antique hand axes. You won't find her collection on display. However, she knows where each and every axe is hidden, and she can reach one in a flash.

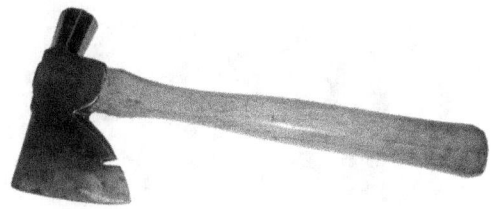

Beretta Modelo 418: Amber Lansden's gun is a rare classic from the pre-WWII period. The Beretta Modelo 418 fires a .25 ACP caliber bullet and is described as an easily concealed "pocket gun". It originated in 1919 and continued in production until the '50s. The small Beretta was the favored pistol of James Bond, up until the novel *Dr. No* in 1958, when it was replaced by the Walther PPK.

Beretta Storm: Parker McGovern, an old school cop, carries a new school weapon—a Beretta Px4 Storm built for police and special duty use. According to Beretta the Px4 Storm is the most advanced sidearm of its kind emphasizing maximum firepower (.45 ACP) in an ergonomic package. The Storm has an overall length of 7.7 inches but, thanks to modern thermoplastic materials, weighs only 28.2 ounces. With one in the chamber and a full magazine, the gun holds 10 rounds.

Beretta Tomcat: The Beretta Tomcat pistol's tip-up barrel makes this tiny weapon the perfect gun for the Cornerman. With it a single bullet can be inserted directly into the barrel. The magazine holds seven rounds of .32 ACP caliber ammunition, but the street corner don prefers to use the weapon as a single-shot pistol. The handgun is tiny (4.9" overall length, 1.1" wide, 3.5" tall and weighs only 15 ounces). It disappears in the big pockets of the Cornerman's jeans.

Beretta Vertec: Mariko Lee's Vertec is a big weapon with a scaled down grip for shooters with smaller hands. The weapon is a 9mm automatic weighing 33.86 ounces. Its magazine holds 10 rounds giving it a loaded capacity of 11 rounds by keeping a round in the chamber. The handgun has an overall length of 8.54 inches.

Cobra C32 Derringer: Rollins' initial backup gun was intentionally destroyed prior to the beginning of the Puppeteer story. The .32 caliber gun is only 2.4 inches long. It weighs 9.5 ounces and has a capacity of two rounds.

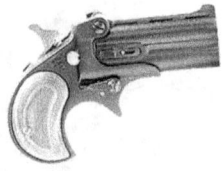

Dickson Special Agent: Sarah Rollins also has a small pistol, a Spanish .32 automatic that is usually locked away. It is a pocket gun that she can easily carry in her jeans or in her purse when prudence dictates doing so. The Dickson is no longer manufactured and is typical of the inexpensive "Saturday night specials" that flooded the U.S in the '50s. Inexpensive or not, the small lightweight handgun proved to be a reliable and comfortable weapon for Mark Rollins' wife.

Kimber Ultra Crimson Carry II: It was Paul Tillman's Kimber that drew first blood in the showdown with Rollins and his team. The automatic fires a .45 ACP caliber bullet out powering the .380 caliber Sig carried by Rollins or Mariko's 9mm EMP. Tillman's Kimber was 6.8 inches long. The gun's light weight, 25 ounces, results from the use of aluminum for the frame material. Crimson trace laser grips give the powerful weapon deadly accuracy.

Sig Sauer P232: Rollins' choice to replace his 9mm Taurus is a Sig Sauer P232 with a laser sight. The handgun fires a .380 cartridge, sometimes called a short 9mm. The handgun has a seven-round magazine, five less than the Taurus it replaced, but it has the advantage of weighing only 17.6 ounces. The weapon is 6.6 inches long and 4.7 inches in height.

Smith & Wesson J Frame: Unable to find the perfect replacement for his derringer, Mark Rollins selected a popular 1950 handgun from his personal armory to serve as his backup weapon—a .38 Chief's Special. This five-shot revolver has serious stopping power but has been labeled a "belly gun" because of its reputation as being inaccurate beyond contact distances. In Rollins' hands the J Frame can deliver five rounds in a tight 2-inch circle at 40 yards.

Smith & Wesson .38 Military and Police Revolver: The standard duty issue Smith & Wesson .38 owned by Paul Tillman was a family hand-me-down originally owned by Tillman's patrolman grandfather. Eventually renamed the Smith & Wesson Model 10, the handgun started life in 1899 as the Military and Police Revolver. This .38 is still the primary duty weapon for many police departments including the New York State Department of Corrections.

Springfield EMP: Mariko's personal armory includes two handguns, the Beretta Vertec and a Springfield EMP, both 9mm handguns. The EMP is an ultra-light compact handgun and is the gun Mariko carries near the end of *Mark Rollins and the Puppeteer*. Fully loading the magazine of an automatic takes lots of finger strength and is the likely reason Mariko always under loads her handguns. She usually loads each with six personal defense rounds. The actual loaded capacity of the EMP is 10 rounds—one in chamber and nine in its magazine. The EMP advantage is its lightweight and small size—23 ounces with an overall length of 6.6 inches.

Swiss Army Field Master: Mark Rollins does not walk out his door every morning carrying a handgun. Unless there is a real and tangible threat to Rollins or those around him, the only weapon you will find on his person is what his daughter Meg calls his "MacGyver" knife, a Swiss Army Field Master.

Tactical Baton: Tony Caruso is reported to own a 9mm Glock but prefers to carry an expandable tactical baton from ASP, Inc. According to Tony, the problem with a handgun is that it is deadly force that you are not going to use unless you are actually under fire. One doesn't have the same reluctance about using a baton—you can render a bad guy completely helpless by breaking his wrist or shattering his kneecap with a single blow without putting innocent bystanders at risk.

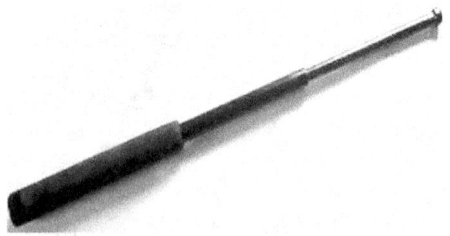

TAR-21: The distinctive TAR-21 used by the Painter is quickly replacing the Uzi as Hollywood's favorite weapon in action flicks making this sexy weapon the logical choice for Mark Rollins' would-be assassin. The name stands for

"Tavor Assault Rifle - 21st Century". It is chambered for 5.56x45mm NATO ammunition. Within the next few years the TAR-21 is expected to become the standard Israeli infantry weapon.

Taurus PT111: Mark Rollins' 9mm Taurus PT111 is constructed of polymer and steel and weighs in at 24 ounces. It is just over six inches long and has a capacity of 13 rounds—12 in the magazine and one in the chamber. Rollins explains that the gun, which was used in his adventure *Mark Rollins and the Rainmaker*, was destroyed in an FBI furnace designed to make guns with a past disappear.

Walther PPK: Tony Caruso, an excellent marksman, uses a rented PPK at the gun range. A Walther PPK pistol is James Bond's signature gun in most of the films portraying the fictional secret agent. Ian Fleming's choice of the Walther PPK directly influenced its modern popularity and its notoriety. Actually the PPK was one of the first successful double-action semi-automatic pistols and a popular weapon of WWII. It is small, easily concealed and fires a .32 caliber cartridge.

9 780982 589809